CHOICES FOR THE MANAGER

CHOICES FOR THE MANAGER

ROSEMARY STEWART

Oxford Centre for Management Studies

Prentice-Hall, Inc., Englewood Cliffs, New Jersey 07632

Library of Congress Cataloging in Publication Data

STEWART, ROSEMARY.
    Choices for the manager.

    Includes bibliographical references and index.
    1. Industrial management—Decision making.   2. Management—Decision making.   I. Title.
HD30.23.S73   658.4'03   81–15321
ISBN 0-13-133173-6   AACR2

Printed in the United States of America

10 9 8 7 6 5 4 3 2 1

ISBN 0-13-133173-6

Prentice-Hall International, Inc., *London*
Prentice-Hall of Australia Pty. Limited, *Sydney*
Prentice-Hall of Canada, Ltd., *Toronto*
Prentice-Hall of India Private Limited, *New Delhi*
Prentice-Hall of Japan, Inc., *Tokyo*
Prentice-Hall of Southeast Asia Pte. Ltd., *Singapore*
Whitehall Books Limited, *Wellington, New Zealand*

Contents

CONTENTS

Preface

My aim in *Choices for the Manager* is the ambitious one of trying to change how the reader thinks about managerial work. I believe this to be necessary because the language commonly used for talking about managerial work takes too little account of what managers actually do. It is often too general, treating managing as primarily a common activity, and also too formal and idealistic, hence divorced from reality. This is not just an academic problem, but more importantly affects the utility of job descriptions used to help in selection and the way that many human resource managers talk about selection, appraisals and training. I am providing a new way of thinking about the nature and the diversity of managerial jobs and about how individuals actually do them. I have developed this as a result of a number of research projects spread over fifteen years and from testing these ideas in management programs designed to help managers to look afresh at their jobs and at how they do them.

A central argument of this book is that all managerial jobs offer some choice in *what* is done as well as in *how* it is done. The latter has received a lot of attention from those interested in management style and leadership, but the former has been curiously neglected. My studies, which have included observation of managers in similar jobs, have highlighted the extent and nature of the differences in the work that is done. In some jobs the differences are so great that managers in similar jobs can and do spend much of their time doing different kinds of work. The existence of choice in managerial work has important implications for the way that we should look at jobs whether as teachers, researchers, human resource managers or as individual managers looking at our own jobs. Unless we recognize both the opportunities for choice that exist in all managerial jobs, and the distinctive nature of the choices in different kinds of job, we cannot adequately understand what managerial work is like. The first chapter of the book describes a new and simple framework for understanding managerial work and behavior that takes account both of the job and of the individual jobholder. The book is then divided into three parts and appendices. Part I explains the opportunities that different jobs offer for individuals to do the job in their own way. There are illustrations from a wide variety of managerial jobs in industry, commerce and the public services. The core of the book is about this opportunity for choice, and its significance for understanding managerial jobs, for considering ways of improving effectiveness and for trying to match the needs of the job and the inclinations of the individual. Part II turns from the description of jobs to the individual jobholder. It shows how individuals differ in the ways in which they see their jobs.

The first chapter in Part III describes different dimensions for comparing jobs that can be useful for selection, appraisal and training. The last three chapters discuss the implications of the book for the academic as teacher and researcher, for the individual manager and for the organization. Appendix 1 is for the academic, it describes the different research studies and discusses methodology. Appendix 2 illustrates how this new way of looking at jobs can be used to make job descriptions more realistic. Appendix 3 gives nine exercises that have been developed and extensively tested in training programs for middle and senior executives from widely different kinds of organization. These will be of use both to teachers and to the individual manager wishing to improve his or her own effectiveness.

This book is addressed to all those who need to understand managerial jobs and managerial behavior. They include the individual manager who is reviewing the work of subordinates, or his or her own approach to the job. They include also the general manager in deciding the managerial selection, training and career policies of the organization and personnel and training managers in developing and applying such policies. Academics need to understand managerial work and behavior, too, if their teaching and research is to be related to reality.

Acknowledgements

This book was only made possible by the help, cooperation and interest of large numbers of people. My chief debt is to my research associates who worked on the different research projects on which this book is based. Phil Long was the full-time research associate for two years on the classifying choices project. Judi Marshall was the part-time research associate on the study of managers' perceptions of choice in their jobs. Peter Smith, Jenny Blake and Pauline Wingate were the part-time research associates on the study of the job of the district administrator in the U.K. national health service. My debt to the researchers on the latter two projects is acknowledged in previous publications, so a special tribute is due to Phil Long who worked on the longest and in many ways the hardest of the three studies, and who carried out a grueling fieldwork programme with persistence and good humour.

This book would not exist but for the cooperation of the companies, the managers and the administrators who took part in the different studies. I am most appreciative of their help and interest and for the time they gave to the studies.

The Social Science Research Council financed two of the three studies, the classifying choices study, and the one on perceptions of choice. They also funded their predecessor. The King Edward's Hospital Fund for London commissioned and financed the study of the district administrator. I am grateful to both bodies for their support.

The framework for understanding managerial work and behaviour that was developed and used in the studies was also tested in twelve two-week managerial programmes at the Oxford Centre for Management Studies and in six two-day seminars. The aim of both was to help managers to take a fresh look at their jobs and how they did them. Peter Smith and Bill Weinstein worked with me on the longer programmes and I much enjoyed and benefitted from their interest and help. Peter Smith's interest in, and contribution to, the research ideas as they have developed over the years has extended far beyond our work together on one of the research projects and on the courses, so I am especially indebted to him. I am indebted, too, to Norman Venus with whom I worked on the two-day seminars for the Chemical and Allied Products Training Board and who contributed a great deal to developing the exercises given in Appendix 2 and to the use of the research ideas for management training.

I am also indebted to those who commented upon the book in draft and who have done a lot to improve it. The defects that remain are solely my responsibility. In the U.K. I am indebted to John Hales of the Training Services Agency, and to John Knibbs for their very detailed suggestions; to Pat Torrie and Norman Venus. In the U.S.A. I am indebted to John Kotter, Dick Osborn and Chet Schriesheim. The final burden of completing the book has been born with great efficiency and unfailing good humor by my secretary, Ann Bond.

1.

Managerial jobs in practice: A framework for understanding them

The people who are doing the job, whether it is at the coal face or in the branch of a bank, are not actually doing what the book says that they should. They may be achieving approximately the same result; frequently doing it better than the book says, but sometimes skipping it and doing it in a slip-shod way. But nevertheless they have adapted it to themselves, how they like to work, how they like to behave, how it looks to them and sometimes what they think the organisation wants. It can be quite different from what it really wants. So that, just as the people in a state have a great capacity for getting out from under and finding ways round things, so the people in an enterprise have an equal capacity for getting out from under and sorting things out to suit themselves.

Lord Armstrong (1977)

The quotation is the voice of experience from a former head of the British Civil Service. Too many of the writings on management have ignored such experience. It is odd that management, which is necessarily a pragmatic art, has attracted such theoretical writing even among those whose task is to analyse jobs for organizations. Most people would accept what Lord Armstrong said: that people exercise choice in how they do their jobs. Yet, curiously, we do not pay this fact of choice the attention that it deserves, either as managers of staff, as personnel managers professionally concerned with the nature of jobs, or when looking at how we do our own jobs. Many managers do not recognize either that they make choices or that they are in a position where they could do so.

This book will take Lord Armstrong's account as a starting point and explore its implications for our understanding of the reality of managerial work and behaviour. It will argue that to understand a job one must know both its formal description and how it can actually be done in practice. The job limits what behaviour is possible, and the incumbent's behaviour helps to define what the job is really like. This flexibility is important because it permits

1

different jobholders to interpret the job differently. The usual methods for describing a job do not allow for such variations, and so miss its dynamic and flexible character.

The book is based on a number of studies of how managers actually do their jobs and how they see them. These studies are summarized in the table in Appendix 1. An earlier study (Stewart, 1976), described how managerial jobs differ in the demands that they make upon managers. It presented a framework for understanding managerial jobs that is the subject of this chapter. Three later studies developed and applied this framework (Stewart, 1979; Stewart *et al.*, 1980; Marshall and Stewart, 1981). These included lengthy interviews about their jobs with managers in different functions and organizations, interviews with their bosses, and observations of managers in similar jobs to identify the different ways in which they did them. The information from these studies was supplemented and tested in numerous courses and seminars with managers, which used the framework described in this chapter to help them to review the nature of their jobs and their approach to them.

The framework described

This framework is presented as a way of looking at managerial jobs and at managerial behaviour. It can be helpful in understanding the general nature of managerial jobs and the differences between them, and can be used to analyse a particular job and to consider how an individual does it. The framework can be of value for individual managers thinking about their own effectiveness, and for those who have to select, appraise and train others.

The framework has three categories: demands, constraints, and choices. Their definitions should be noted, as they—and especially the last one, 'choice'—will be used throughout the book.

Demands What anyone in the job *has* to do. There are many things that a manager ought to do because they are in the job description, or because his or her boss thinks them important, but 'demands' is a narrower term: 'demands' are only what *must* be done.

Constraints The factors, internal or external to the organization, that limit what the jobholder can do.

Choices These are the activities that the jobholder can, but does not have to, do. They are the opportunities for one jobholder to do different work from another and to do it in different ways.

Different kinds of demands, constraints, and choices are summarized in

Table 1.1. For some readers the table will be sufficient so they should skip to page 6. Others will prefer to read the explanation that follows.

Demands

Demands are of two kinds—having to do certain kinds of work, and the overall satisfying of certain criteria—although there will be come choices in the way that these are met. In some jobs such criteria are specific, such as the amount of turnover or the volume of units manufactured. In others the criteria may be

Table 1.1 Summary of different kinds of demands, constraints, and choices in managerial jobs

DEMANDS
Overall meeting minimum criteria of performance
Doing certain kinds of work. Such work is determined by:
    The extent to which personal involvement is required in the unit's work
    Who must be contacted and the difficulty of the work relationship
    Contacts' power to enforce their expectations
    Bureaucratic procedures that cannot be ignored or delegated
    Meetings that must be attended

CONSTRAINTS
Resource limitations
Legal and trade union constraints
Technological limitations
Physical location
Organizational constraints, especially extent to which the work of the manager's unit is defined
Attitudes of other people to:
    Changes in systems, procedures, organization, pay, and conditions
    Changes in the goods or services produced
    Work outside the unit

CHOICES
In *how* the work is done (see Chapter 2)
In *what* work is done
    Choices within a defined area:
        To emphasize certain aspects of the job
        To select some tasks and to ignore or delegate others
    Choices in boundary management
    Choices to change the area of work:
        To change the unit's domain
        To develop a personal domain:
            To become an expert
            To share work, especially with colleagues
            To take part in organizational and public activities

very general, but some minimum level of performance will be required, although the time scale in which it is possible to judge this may be a long one. The discussion that follows is about the first kind of demand, the specific work that must be done.

The work that managers must do themselves is determined by the following factors:

– The extent to which they must be personally involved in the work of the unit[1] for which they are responsible
– Whom they must work with and the difficulty of these work relationships
– The expectations that others have of what they should do, and the consequences of not meeting these expectations
– Bureaucratic procedures that cannot be ignored or delegated
– Meetings that must be attended

The demands for a manager's personal involvement in the work of the unit for which he or she is responsible will be determined in part by the power of other people to enforce their expectations of what the manager will do and in part by the need for supervision. A boss, for example, may insist that the subordinate knows operational details, or an important customer may expect to deal with the boss rather than with a subordinate. The need for supervision will depend mainly upon whether subordinates *can* and whether they *will* do their work without the manager's supervision. An earlier study (Stewart, 1976) described these and other factors that determine the demands for supervision.

Managers will have to work with people other than their subordinates. The ways in which jobs vary in their contacts, and in the nature of the demands that these involve, were described in the earlier study. This discussion will not be repeated here, as this book focuses upon the choices in jobs.

Managers work with other people who have expectations about what they will do and how they will do it. The extent to which these expectations are demands that the manager must meet will vary with the individual's power to enforce his expectations. Such power may range from the sanctions that a boss may have to the opportunities that others can have for withholding the cooperation that may be essential for the jobholder to do the job. Both colleagues and subordinates may have such power, and thus be in a position to ensure that some of their expectations are demands upon the manager. The demands upon managers in similar jobs may vary because of differences in the expectations of the people with whom the manager must work and with their relative power *vis-à-vis* the jobholder.

The last two sources of demands listed above require less explanation. All managerial jobs in sizeable organizations involve personally doing some

1. 'Unit' is used for the manager's responsibilities, whether it is for a section, branch, department, area, division, company, school, or hospital.

bureaucratic work. The most common are preparing budgets, authorizing expenditure, and carrying out staff appraisals. Attendance at meetings is listed as a separate source of demands because in some organizations it can be much the most time-consuming.

Constraints

The common constraints that limit a manager's choices are:

– Resource constraints, including buildings
– Legal and trade union constraints
– Technological limitations of equipment and process
– Physical location
– Organizational policies and procedures
– Attitudes that influence what actions other people will accept or tolerate

A major organizational constraint upon the nature of the choices available in a particular job is the extent to which the work to be done by the manager's unit is defined. Some jobs are responsible for a defined area of operation that the manager cannot change, such as the retail chain store manager who must operate within the physical constraints of the store and the company policies for the goods to be sold; the area sales manager who is limited both in the products to be sold and the geographical area and, even more constrained, the melting shop manager in a steel works. Other jobs, like that of a management accountant, have much more open-ended responsibilities.

Attitudes of subordinates, of colleagues, and of the manager's boss may constrain what changes can be made in the unit. They can also constrain the work that the manager can do outside his or her own unit. A manager who has to market goods or services internally or externally may be constrained in changing these by customers' and clients' unwillingness to accept changes in output, whether it is a new product, computer system, training programme, or a different method of determining prices.

Choices

There are choices in the kind of work that is done and in how it is done. This book concentrates mainly upon the former because it is the aspect of managerial work that has been neglected. Much more attention has been paid to *how* managers do their jobs, in such diverse aspects as leadership style and time management. The next seven chapters are about different kinds of choices in *what* work can be done. Chapters 2 and 3 discuss choices that are common to all or most managerial jobs. Chapter 2 includes a short account of the choices in methods of work as well as a longer discussion of the content of work. Chapter 3 describes the choice that exists in most managerial jobs to try

5

and protect one's unit from disturbance, which we shall call 'boundary management'. It is discussed separately from the choices considered in Chapter 2 because its importance merits a chapter to itself. It is important because managers differ widely in the extent to which they exercise this choice, and because in some jobs it can make possible the changes of unit domain that are the subject of Chapter 4. Chapters 4–7 describe choices that are found only in certain kinds of jobs. These chapters discuss the choices that seemed most important in our research and in the course work with managers. It is the recognition of the existence and range of choices in jobs that is important for the argument of this book, rather than their exhaustive description.

A major determinant of the amount and nature of the available choices is the extent to which the work is defined—one of the constraints mentioned above. Such definition prescribes the manager's *domain*, that is the area within which he or she can be active. We found from our studies of managerial jobs that it is helpful for understanding them to distinguish two kinds of domain: the unit for which the manager is responsible, the unit domain; and the possibilities for work outside it, the personal domain. The distinction between the two is not a precise one, but it is useful for highlighting the different kinds of work that a jobholder may be able to do. The management of a unit will usually offer choices of selection (some tasks can be ignored or delegated), and will always offer choices of emphasizing one aspect of the work more than another. Chapter 4 will describe the choices of unit domain, and how the manager in some jobs can change the work that is done by the unit, its output. Chapter 5 will discuss the choices that some jobs offer to do work outside the unit. The different kinds of choices that we identified in the nature of the work that a manager can do are outlined in Table 1.1, together with the demands and constraints that define and limit these choices.

Demands, constraints and choices: the job and the individual

The framework can be used to think about both the nature of a job and how an individual does it. It can also be used to think about the differences between jobs. Jobs will differ in the nature of their demands and in the time and effort that they take up. Jobs can differ, too, in the nature of the constraints and in how much these limit what the jobholder can do. The choices will be limited both by the extent of the demands and by the nature of the constraints. Either or both may considerably limit the choices available. Jobs differ, as we shall see in subsequent chapters, both in the amount and the nature of the choices of work that they offer. Figure 1.1 shows how demands, constraints, and choices vary in two different kinds of job. One has a larger area of demands and a relatively close band of constraints; the second has a small core of demands and, as the line of constraints is also much further out, a larger area of choices. These jobs differ for the individuals doing them and for the requirements for effectiveness. The first is in many ways easier: effectiveness in it is mainly about performing the demands competently, although there is some scope for choice. Effectiveness in the second job is much more about choosing the right thing to do.

The lines in Fig. 1.1 are wavy to suggest the likelihood of change. Changes in either demands or constraints will affect the area of choice. Such changes may arise from the actions of others within the organization, from changes in environmental conditions, or because of what the jobholder does. Individuals may create new demands because of the expectations that they establish by their behaviour. These new demands may remain personal to them or become

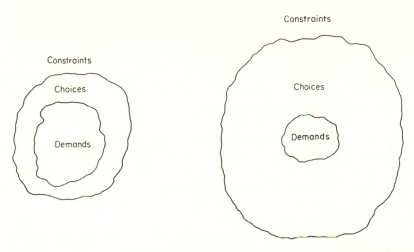

Fig. 1.1 Differences in the demands, constraints, and choices in two jobs

attached to the job so that they will be inherited by their successors. The actions of the jobholder can also affect constraints, as one of the choices in most jobs is to try and find a way round the constraints, or to change their nature. Some constraints are much stronger and harder to change than others, but we should never, as Lord Armstrong pointed out, underrate the individual's capacity to get out from under.

Individuals in similar jobs may have somewhat different demands, constraints, and choices, both in fact and in their perceptions of them. They will differ in fact, because other people's expectations of what they will do may differ, as will their power to enforce their expectations. The choices that managers are able to exercise may also vary with their abilities and experience. Managers in similar jobs also differ, we found, in the demands, constraints, and choices that they *see*. Many will see more demands than there are because they think that most of what they do is a demand, rather than recognizing that

7

some of it is really a choice. They may not realize that they are making choices in the work that they do. Some individuals will also see more demands than others because they interpret other people's expectations as being more demanding. One can also create additional demands by choices that one makes, such as agreeing to serve on a committee. Managers differ, too, in their perception of constraints. Some see themselves as more constrained that others because they exaggerate the extent to which other people's attitudes limit what they can do, or the need to adhere strictly to policies and procedures. Individuals' interpretations of demands and constraints will in turn affect the amount and kind of choices that are available to them. In Chapter 11, on implications for the individual, we shall suggest how managers can seek to increase the choices available to them. They may be able to modify the demands or the constraints so as to increase the actual choices that are available, or they may change their view of demands and constraints and so their perception of the available choices.

Delegation as an illustration of demands, constraints and choices

Most managers in charge of subordinates have some choice in the amount of delegation and in what they delegate. 'Most' rather than 'all', because there are some jobs, such as retail chain store superintendents, where there is little choice. Managers' choices in delegation will be limited by the demands, that is by the work that they must do themselves, either because they are not permitted to delegate it, such as signing expense forms, or because the expectations that they, rather than their subordinates, will do it are too strong to make delegation politically feasible. The extent of these demands varies considerably between different jobs. In some there is wide flexibility in how the work is shared between boss and subordinates; in others there are strong demarcations between the work that is done at different levels.

A manager's choice of delegation can be constrained in many ways. There are constraints imposed by the common tendency for customers to go to the most senior person that they can: such constraints can often be overcome. There may be constraints from the limited knowledge and experience of subordinates. There can be status constraints, too, which mean that some work is more easily done by the boss than by the next level down in the hierarchy. And there is a less obvious constraint: the lack of opportunities for other work for the managers who do delegate a lot. Some jobs, as we shall illustrate in Chapter 5, offer very wide opportunities for managers to do work other than manage their own units, while others offer little or none. In the latter the concern expressed by some managers—'if I delegate a lot I will be working myself out of a job'—will be true at least in terms of genuinely having enough to do, if not of ceasing to have a job. This has proved a problem in a few job enrichment plans, where job enrichment has meant job impoverishment for the boss.

Managers' choice of delegation can also be constrained by their perception of the situation. They may see their subordinates as less capable than they are. They may consider their lack of experience a bar to delegation rather than as a temporary constraint that can be overcome. They may think that they must always personally respond to customers. They may believe that they must be able to answer any detailed question that their boss asks.

In summary, jobs differ in the demands and constraints that limit the choice of delegation, and individuals differ in their perception of the choices that are available. Neither of these facts is adequately recognized in discussions on delegation.

Uses of the framework

Demands, constraints, and choices can be used to understand any kind of managerial job, and other jobs as well. The framework is useful because it provides a different way of thinking about jobs and about how individuals do them. In selection it can help in analysing what a job is really like. This way of analysing a job highlights the training needs for jobs offering different kinds of choice. The framework can help in appraising how an individual does a job by enabling the appraiser to consider what is distinctive about the subordinates' approach and to review how well this is matched to the needs of the job at that time. Individual managers can use demands, constraints, and choices as a way of thinking about their job and of examining their approach to it. The justification for these claims will be considered in Part Three.

Summary

A framework was described for thinking about managerial jobs in general, and for understanding particular jobs and how individuals do them. It consists of three parts: 'demands', which anyone on the job *has* to do, cannot get away with not doing; 'constraints', the factors that limit what the jobholder can do; and 'choices', the activities that the jobholder can, but does not have to, do. Demands, constraints, and choices are dynamic because they change over time. The merit of this way of looking at jobs and at how people do them is that it takes into account the fact that people do jobs in their own way, both in what they do and in how they do it.

The factors that create demands and constraints and the kinds of choices that exist in jobs were broadly described. There are choices that are found in all or most managerial jobs, such as emphasizing one aspect of the job more than another and taking actions to protect the unit for which one is responsible from disturbance. Then there are choices that exist in a smaller number of jobs, such as changing the work that is done by one's unit. Some jobs also offer a choice to become involved in other work within the organization or outside it. In jobs offering a lot of choice individuals in similar jobs can spend much of their time on different kinds of work. Delegation was used to illustrate demands, constraints, and choices.

PART ONE

The common and distinctive choices in managerial jobs

The aim of Part One is to discuss the main choices in jobs that we identified in our researches. Chapter 2 describes choices that are common to managerial jobs. Chapter 3 is about a choice that exists in most, but not all, managerial jobs; that of trying to protect the unit for which one is responsible from outside interferences. Chapters 4–7 discuss less commonly available choices of domain; that is, the area within which the jobholder can work.

2.

Common choices in managerial jobs

People, as Lord Armstrong pointed out, adapt jobs to themselves. Managerial jobs provide plenty of scope for such adaptation. An understanding of the nature of the flexibility inherent in all managerial jobs is necessary if we are to have a realistic picture of what they are like. This chapter describes the kind of choices that exist in all or most managerial jobs. It does not attempt to give an exhaustive classification of all the common choices that exist. Rather, its purpose is to describe and illustrate the extent and variety of these choices. The account of choices in the content of work is more comprehensive than that of choices of methods, because the latter can be described in so many different ways.

In this and Chapters 3–7 we are describing the choices that exist and are not assessing whether their exercise makes for effectiveness: the implications for effectiveness are discussed in Chapters 11 and 12.

Choices in *what* work is done

Choices of emphasis

There are two basic options. One can either do the job as an engineer or as an administrator.

Production engineer

Managers in similar jobs will spend some of their time on different activities. In the more clearly defined and routinized jobs the main difference will be in the amount of time devoted to particular aspects of the job. This is a choice of emphasis. The particular nature of the choice will vary in different jobs. One of the most common is that given in the quotation from the production engineer.[1] Managers who have had a specialist training have a choice of

1. The academic reader may want to know the nature of some of the generalizations made. The statements 'any', 'all', 'many', and 'most' mean, unless specifically modified, that, from the evidence of the different researches and from the courses on managerial work, this generalization appears to be justified. The generalization is worded more cautiously where it is thought that a study of other kinds of managers in the UK or elsewhere might produce different results.

emphasizing that aspect of their work and even of getting involved in technical questions when they do not officially form part of the job.

Any post in charge of subordinates offers a choice of emphasis, both in the amount of time spent on supervision and in what aspects of supervision are stressed. There is always some choice in leadership style, even if the company climate does not permit a manager to follow a natural bent for autocracy. There is a choice, too, in the attention that is paid to different aspects of supervision such as monitoring performance, training and development, or welfare. Managers can, within the constraints imposed by the expectations of boss and subordinates and the customs of the organization, choose to do different kinds of supervisory work and to do it in different ways.

Another opportunity for choice of emphasis that exists in most managerial jobs is that of *liaison*, that is, establishing and maintaining cooperative relations with people in other parts of the organization, or outside it, who are likely to be useful. There is more scope for this choice in jobs that require or permit a wide range of contacts than in those where contacts are mainly limited to one's boss and one's own staff. One aspect of this choice is examined in Chapter 3 in boundary management.

One of the choices that all managers can exercise is in how they divide their time between different people. Even in a job with a narrow range of contacts, there is still some choice available in the amount of time spent with different subordinates. Jobs with a wide range of contacts can offer much more choice: the manager may be able to choose the amount of time and attention that is focused downwards, upwards, sideways, or outwards to people outside the organization. A simple count of the amount of time that an individual spends with different types of contacts can help to show where attention is being focused.

In the earlier study (Stewart, 1976) 12 contact types were identified according to the way in which a manager's time was divided between different categories of contacts: boss, subordinates, people in other departments, and contacts outside the organization. When the earlier book was written the contact types were seen as demands that necessarily characterize different types of jobs. However, later research showed that this is true only of some jobs; in others people have a choice between two or more contact types. The contact types are a convenient way of summarizing how a manager divides his or her time between different categories of contacts. Readers who are interested are referred to the earlier book; here we shall only give examples of how choices of emphasis are shown by the amount of time spent with different groups of people.

The way that two plant managers divided their contact time is shown in Table 2.1. Plant manager A spent much more time with his subordinates than with people in other parts of the organization. He saw his job as concerned primarily with man management and with contributing his technical knowledge to the technical problems that arose. His main focus of attention was downwards. Plant manager B had a very different approach to, and view of, the job. He left his subordinates to run much of the operations themselves. He had satisfied himself of their ability to do so, and saw his main task as ensuring that they got the services and supplies that they needed. He also spent some time working with other plant managers and with plant engineers on mutual problems, and contacted suppliers to discuss possible technical innovations.

The choice of a primarily downwards focus of attention, illustrated by plant manager A, or of a more sideways and outwards one exists in many managerial jobs. How much choice there is will, however, vary in different jobs and at different times in the same job.

Table 2.1   Examples of the distribution of contact time by two plant managers in the same works

	Plant manager A %	Plant manager B %
Subordinates	70	40
Boss	6	6
Other departments	24	51
External	0	3
	100	100

The motivation of subordinates, or their level of technical competence, may make it essential for the manager to devote more of his or her time to them. The opportunities for choice are also likely to vary with how long the manager has been in the job, and with how long the subordinates have been in theirs. Some of the managers that we interviewed for the research described the different options that existed for them at different stages of their job. They reported that someone new in a job may need to spend more time with subordinates to assess their competence and approach to the job and to train them if necessary. Once this is done the manager is free to turn his or her attention to other problems. A manager who has a constant succession of new subordinates will have much less choice, especially if they are inexperienced.

The nature of the technology may also affect the choices that exist in a manager's pattern of contacts. Interviews carried out in a large chemical works showed that many of the production and engineering jobs offered a wide choice in the relative emphasis given to working with subordinates compared with working with colleagues. The widespread nature of the choice in this company probably reflects the high calibre of subordinates and the interdependence of the technology.

Discussions with a number of marketing managers, working for the same organization, each having two or three product managers responsible to them, showed a variation in the time spent with subordinates compared with peers that was similar to the plant managers. Such a marked variation is more surprising in jobs with only a few subordinates. It illustrates the variety of jobs that offer this choice of emphasis.

Choices of selection of work

All managerial jobs offer a choice of emphasizing different aspects. Many also offer some choice of selection between different kinds of work, so that some aspects of the job can be given considerable time and attention and others can be ignored or delegated. Here we seek only to illustrate common choices of selection. Later chapters will describe distinctive choices that characterize particular jobs. One possibility, for example, is to play little or no attention to staff development, though in some organizations senior management's expectations that all their managers will do so may preclude such a choice.

The more diverse the tasks of the manager, the greater usually will be the possibilities of choice between them, both of emphasis and of selection. A good example of such a diverse job, though one that has more constraints on the work that can be done than those we shall consider in Chapter 3, is that of the hotel manager in a chain of hotels. The key tasks for hotel managers in one chain were given in very general terms as:

– Maintaining standards
– Employing the right staff
– Meeting the profit target

A more detailed set of key tasks could be, and in some hotel chains is, provided. These tasks give little clue to what a hotel manager may actually do, or to what the choices are. An area director in this chain gave a more informative description when he illustrated the diversity of the job. 'The hotel manager', he said, 'is expected to be hotelier, caterer, accountant, personnel officer, and publicity agent, to have housekeeping talents, skills in design and decor and in maintenance.' He did not include the leadership skills that many may think are essential to the running of a successful hotel. The choices of emphasis and of selection in such a diverse job are considerable, allowing scope, even in a chain with highly formalized policies, for individuals with different interests to pursue them. All hotel managers will have to pay attention to financial management, as profit figures will be one of the major criteria by which they are assessed. Even so, individuals can differ in the emphasis that they give to financial management. There is a choice of encouraging staff to develop special expertise, which can also be used to allow the manager to spend little or no time on that part of the job. The manager can choose to take a special interest in catering and to encourage innovation both in menus and in the groups for which special catering is done. The job offers other opportunities for individuals with different interests to pursue them. The more mechanically minded can spend time on maintenance problems; those who are not can delegate that aspect. Design and decor offer choices for the artistically inclined to develop a congenial area of work. Managers who are not interested may consult head office specialists more, or encourage a sub-ordinate to develop skills there.

Delegation is one of the ways by which a manager can exercise choices of emphasis and of selection. Such choices may also be exercised without delegation because the manager may naturally do certain kinds of work and not others without considering who should do it, or even whether it should be done at all. An example of a selection choice that may be instinctive or planned is promoting the value of one's work and that of one's staff. Some managers are such natural salesmen that they may do this to anyone they meet; a few will do it as a conscious policy of trying to impress those whose opinion they think is important. An illustration of this comes from our observation of two maintenance managers who worked for a large local authority. They were each observed for a week during which a visit was paid to their depot by a local councillor. One of the managers spent no time preparing for the visit. The other devoted most of the previous morning to doing so. He gave instructions about the refreshments for lunch, about what his subordinates should be doing and the impression that they should be seeking to create. His objective was to stress the non-routine aspects of the work, so that its importance was enhanced and, with that, the status of the department. He was keen, he said, to correct the 'grease can' image of maintenance.

Maintenance or innovation

One form of selection is the interest taken in innovation. Most managerial jobs offer at least some choice in whether the manager focuses upon trying to keep the unit's work on an even keel, or is also looking for opportunities for improvement and development. The nature and extent of opportunities for innovation vary widely from one job to another; so does the importance of stability. Some jobs, particularly many of those in production management and in the more routine service jobs, are primarily concerned with maintaining stability. In a few jobs there may be no need for innovation and little opportunity for it. The aim of some jobs, particularly those in research and development, is innovation. Between these two extremes of stability or innovation as the primary goal come most managerial jobs. These offer a choice in whether, and if so the extent to which, and the directions in which, the jobholder looks for ways of improving what is done.

Observation of managers shows a marked difference between them in the interest that they take in innovation. In some jobs, for example production

17

management and retail chain store management, managers will usually spend time walking round the area for which they are responsible. However, what they are actually doing then can vary considerably. One manager may use such tours primarily for purposes of motivation; even then, there are differences between those who are seeking to establish friendly relations with their staff and those who are primarily checking up on what is being done. Another manager may be always on the look out for ways of improving layout or methods of working.

The difference between two managers in similar jobs can be illustrated by two production superintendents who worked for the same company. Both had been in their job for some years. They were describing their approach to their job and answering questions about the opportunities for choice that they had. One described his approach as follows:

I have to plan my week. First morning and evening I check on current production. I divide the rest of my day equally between current events, tomorrow's and next year's events, but I have to be careful that I'm not spending too much time away from the things that I must look after; too much time thinking about the future and not enough time looking at today.

The other said:

Most of my day is taken up either chasing shortages or design problems that have cropped up. There is little scope for choice. My job is a bit routine in that it reproduces the same problems for a large number of years and once you've found the best way of doing it, you try and stick to it.

The difference between the two managers may be partly explained by differences in what they were producing. The safety considerations for the second production superintendent were greater than for the first; he, therefore, had an additional constraint upon innovation. However, the difference also reflected the ways that they did their jobs, that is the choices that they took.

Some jobs offer more choice of innovation because they are divided between a maintenance and an innovative part. This is true, for example, of the personnel jobs that are responsible for operating current policies, for contributing to the development of new ones and for keeping up to date with thinking on personnel matters. Yet personnel managers may choose to spend all their time in administering policies and procedures, firefighting and perhaps counselling. Someone who works like that may leave the job, and the personnel position in their part of the organization, much as they found it, as they have not sought to improve it. In most personnel jobs there is this longer-term more innovative component. Often this is not a demand, but something that the individual may make time for or not; hence a choice.

Many of the jobs in management services are good examples of a wide choice between stability and innovation. Usually there is considerable choice in the attention paid to innovation and the form that innovation takes. There is innovation in equipment; working in an area where the manufacturers frequently produce new products and new software, the manager will have a choice in the interest taken in these new developments, and in the time spent with computer manufacturers and at professional meetings. There will be a choice, too, in the attention that the manager gives to encouraging, and looking for, new uses for the computer. The job may offer such a wide choice between stability and innovation that different jobholders can spend much of their time on different kinds of work. One manager may focus attention mainly upon ensuring that the department runs smoothly, that the staff are well trained and well motivated, and that the users get a prompt and reliable service. Another may spend much of the time on innovation in equipment and systems design.

Even in jobs that offer fewer opportunities for innovation, there can still be a choice. The boss of a fleet buyer described it thus:

He could follow the rules and regulations, not looking to left or right, or he could try to find new ways of buying the cars and of getting better terms. He could buy different models and look for different suppliers.

The opportunities for choice in innovation differ both between jobs and at different periods in the same job. The boss of a chief financial accountant described the constraints on innovation as follows:

He is circumscribed by sophisticated computer systems so has limited choice. He has to learn to live within the monster and can only refine the fringes, not the core. He has inherited a well-managed area where most of the innovation has already occurred.

However, the speaker had previously had that job so may have used all the possibilities for innovation that he saw and not recognized others that existed.

The changes that are taking place within the organization or outside it will affect the opportunities for innovation in a job. There are more opportunities for innovation where there are rapid technological developments, as we saw for managers of management services. The development of computer facilities within a company may also open up new opportunities for innovation for managers in other departments who can take an interest in computerized systems. The computer has been one of the factors making for change, both opening up new possibilities and, as for the financial accountant mentioned above, reducing others. Changes in company structures may also open up opportunities for innovation, such as developing new accounting controls and systems. There are many ways in which the opportunities for innovation may change. Even where there is little change, some choice of looking for, and initiating, at least modest innovations is likely to exist.

19

Choices in risk taking

There may be some managerial jobs that are so formalized that one cannot choose to avoid or to take risks, but most offer such a choice even if only in staff selection. In the jobs that we studied we found none where the jobholder or the boss, and often both, thought that there was not such a choice. Clearly, the opportunities for this vary considerably between jobs. Some jobs are primarily about risk-taking; others about risk-avoiding. Even in these there is a choice in the degree to which this purpose is pursued.

One problem in discussing opportunities for choice in risk-taking is that there are so many different kinds of risks. It is not useful to seek to enumerate them all, but it is necessary to recognize that, when people talk about risk-taking, they may mean very different things. A broad distinction can be made between business risks, where failure will cost the organization money, and organizational risks. The former can be illustrated by the boss who said:

He can choose to take risks provided I do not hear of them. If he chooses to avoid a risk, he misses business opportunities.

Sales manager's boss

The latter can be illustrated by the production superintendent who said:

I'll make my own freedom. I bend the rules to give me the freedom and every rule is there to be broken or bent or twisted, isn't it? I take the philosophy that it's far better to be criticized for doing something than criticized for not doing something, whether or not at the end of the day you make a terrible hash of it.

In most organizations there is a choice of bucking the system, of finding ways round official policies and procedures. Usually the larger and more formalized the organization, the more opportunities there are for this choice.

The hotel manager's job is one that offers a variety of choices to take business risks. There are immediate financial ones, like cashing cheques for known customers. There are others that may have a more indirect effect on the business, such as overbooking. Both of these are decisions that the manager can choose not to make, though such a choice can carry a business cost. There are other decisions that have to be made and that can carry risk, such as what to do about a guest's misconduct.

A choice that exists in many jobs, particularly those where there are risky decisions to be taken, is to try and avoid personal risk by consultation. Many personnel management jobs offer such a choice, particularly those operating in a difficult industrial relations climate. The manager can often opt for a safe way of running the job by referring difficult industrial relations decisions upwards, by not proposing changes, by trying not to make recommendations that could be risky without involving others, by sticking to the rules, and by hiding behind company policies rather than risk antagonizing recalcitrant managers or shop stewards.

An individual's attitude to risk, and willingness to take it, may be influenced by whether doing so will expose him or her to being personally identified with the mistake. Some jobs are more exposed than others to such personal risk, and may or may not offer a choice of seeking to avoid it by sharing the decision.

How these choices vary

The extent of the opportunities for exercising these common choices will vary in different jobs, and in similar jobs in different companies. They may also vary at different times in the same job. These variations will be determined by the demands and constraints that limit and define the choice that is available. Some of these arise, as we have seen, from the kind of job; others from changes in the situation of the company or of the job.

Rapid changes in the size of an organization, either upwards or downwards, may well impose additional demands and constraints, as well as sometimes opening up new opportunities for choice. Rapid expansion may, for example, impose a demand to spend an unusual amount of time in selection and training. This can be a particular burden on labour-intensive departments like sales, where the district or area sales manager will want to take part in the interviewing. A rapid decline will impose demands to spend more time on organizational decisions and with subordinates, even if much of the redundancy counselling is left to personnel.

There are a number of other factors that will determine the demands and constraints and hence the opportunities for choice. The success of the unit and of the organization generally will affect the constraints. The manager of a successful unit is likely to be given a freer hand in emphasis and selection between different parts of the job than the head of an unsuccessful one. A shortage of staff of the right number, qualifications, and experience can be a major constraint on the manager's choice of emphasis and selection. A change in the manager's boss can affect both demands and constraints. The production engineer quoted earlier as saying that there was an option between doing the job as an engineer or as an administrator added:

Now that is partly determined for one by the guy that you've got to answer to because that guy's going to ask engineering questions or he's going to ask administrative questions. He is going to ask the when and not the why.

The choices that we described are commonly available, but the manager may also have the choice of trying to increase the extent to which they can be exercised. A common way of doing so is by learning how to manage the boss so that he or she leaves one greater freedom to run the job the way that one

21

wants. Another, which we discuss in the chapter on boundary management, is by trying to limit the disturbances that other departments and those outside the organization can cause.

Choices in how work is done

There are common choices in *how* work is done. The one that has been widely studied is leadership style, so it need not be considered here. There are many other and less commonly recognized choices. The main ones that we noted in our observation of managers in similar jobs were in:

– The amount of fragmentation of the day
– The formality or informality of contacts
– Whether people, especially subordinates, are seen alone, in pairs or in groups
– The time spent in meetings
– The time spent travelling

The culture of the organization and the habits of one's boss can greatly restrict choice in methods of working. In some organizations managers are expected to be always available and, especially in American companies, to have their doors open, or to work in an open plan office. The demand then is for informal contacts and a highly fragmented pattern of work. A boss who makes frequent contact and work requests is another factor that limits choice. So, too, are frequent meetings which are customary in many large organizations and some smaller ones.

As far as we could tell, all jobs offer some choice in the extent to which work is fragmented. Managers in some jobs may not be able to control the interruptions of others, but they have a choice in the extent to which they fragment their own work. Some of them, we found, switched from one task to another as they happened to think of something different, rather than trying to complete what they were doing. There is some choice, too, in the extent to which managers seek to plan their day, even though jobs differ widely in how easy or difficult it will be for them to keep to a plan. However, one person in a job may say that it is quite impossible to do so, and another in a similar job may choose to make it possible for at least some of the time.

There are jobs that offer a wide choice in methods of working. Our observation of 11 district administrators, a senior management post in the National Health Service, showed great variations in the ways in which they organized their time. At one extreme were those who worked behind a closed door marked 'Private' and guarded by a secretary. They spent longish periods alone reading and preparing papers for meetings of the management team. Contacts with others were mainly pre-arranged. At the other extreme were those who worked in an open office with their immediate subordinates nearby. They moved frequently in and out of each other's offices discussing outstanding problems and coping together with any crises. These district administrators were also freely available to other callers. Many of their contacts were spontaneous rather than pre-arranged. The difference between these two extremes was partly in their views of what it was important to do in the job, but they also reflected, in the first, a conscious plan to organize one's time and, in the latter, a primarily reactive and unplanned approach to the job.

These administrators can protect themselves behind a closed door and a secretary. Many managers are not able to do this. Even so, our observation of pairs of managers in similar jobs showed marked differences in their pattern of work, with the exception of the pair of service managers in an American electronics company who worked in an open plan office.

Implications

The general implication is that, to think usefully about a job, whether from the point of view of the organization or of the individual, requires a recognition of the flexibility that exists in all managerial jobs. The implications of this flexibility for the organization in selecting, appraising, and training *managers* will be discussed in Chapter 12, and for the *individual*, in Chapter 11. Here it is worth stressing that there are choices even in jobs with high demands and many constraints. All managerial jobs offer some opportunities for one individual to do the job differently from another. These differences are in what is done as well as in how it is done.

The choices described in Chapters 2 and 3 are like those offered in a table d'hôte menu. One can eat more of one item and less of another; one may even skip a course. In Chapters 4–7 we shall describe à la carte jobs, though in all there will be constraints on the range of choice as there are in any menu; the items that are on offer will vary in different jobs as they do in different restaurants. In some jobs the range of choice will be pretty limited.

Summary

This chapter described the kind of choices that exist in all or most managerial jobs. These are summarized in Table 2.2. We noted that the extent of these choices and their particular character will vary in different jobs, organizations, and over time. Despite these variations, there is a general implication: to understand managerial jobs one must recognize that they provide opportunities for jobholders to distribute their time differently between different activities, to do some things and not others, and to do the job in different ways. In sum: managerial jobs offer choices in what is done and how. They are flexible.

Table 2.2 Summary of common choices in managerial jobs

CHOICES IN WHAT IS DONE; THE CONTENT OF WORK
In the relative emphasis given to different parts of the job: e.g.,
    To its technical aspects
    To supervision, and to the different aspects of supervision
    In the time spent with people other than subordinates

In selecting between different kinds of work, doing some tasks that
another might not do, and ignoring or delegating others:
    The attention given to innovation
    Boundary management (Chapter 3)
In risk-taking and its kind and extent

CHOICES IN HOW WORK IS DONE; THE METHODS OF WORK
In the amount of fragmentation of the day
In the formality or informality of contacts
In whether people, especially subordinates, are seen alone, in pairs, or in groups
In the time spent in meetings
In the time spent travelling

There are many other choices in how work is done, most notably leadership style

The organization's policies and customs will help to determine how much choice
there is in the methods of work

3.

Boundary management

You should always be thinking who can screw your department up.

Service manager

I think the name of the game here is carving out manoeuvring room for yourself.

Manager, profit centre providing internal specialist service

In the previous chapter we described selection between different kinds of work as one of the common choices in managerial jobs. In this chapter we discuss a choice of work that is found in many managerial jobs. It is worth highlighting in a separate chapter because managers do not always give it the attention that it merits. It is illustrated in the quotations above. In Chapters 4–7 we shall examine choices of selection that are found in a more limited number of jobs.

Both managers were thinking about how those outside their unit could affect its work, and what they could do to avert such disturbances and constraints. We shall call that 'boundary management'. Managers who are aware of this choice will seek to maintain or to improve the conditions within which the unit operates. Their efforts may need to be focused upon their boss, other senior managers, staff and service departments, suppliers and customers, whether inside or outside the organization, government officials, trade union officers, and community pressure groups. Any of these may, depending upon the job, be able to limit the manager's freedom to maintain or develop the unit.

This choice is especially interesting for management development because we found marked differences between managers in whether they recognized its existence, and, if they did, in the attention that they gave it, and in how they approached it. One explanation of the difference is how they saw the environment of their unit: some managers thought of it as imposing demands and constraints that had to be accepted, others as something that could be changed. Another explanation is the manager's focus of attention; whether it was primarily downwards, and concerned with the internal management of the unit, or whether it included the people outside who could affect its operation. A simple guide to the attention that a manager pays to boundary management is the distribution of time between subordinates and all other contacts and, in many jobs, more specifically, the distribution of time between subordinates on the one hand and peers and seniors on the other. This is only a crude guide, because the lateral contacts may be for other purposes, but a manager who spends a large majority of the time with subordinates is unlikely to be interested in boundary management.

Managers who are active in boundary management tend to think differently from those who are not. They are more concerned with trying to predict possible sources of disturbance and with taking preventive action. They think more about the need to influence other people and about the methods they can use to do so. Many of the managers whom we met thought about how best they could get their subordinates to do what they wanted, but only a minority also considered how to influence people in other departments.

Managers who choose to include boundary management as one of their activities use a number of different approaches. Some concentrate on *planning.* Preventive maintenance is an example of a planned approach to the problem of an uneven work load. Many are what Kotter (1982) has called *network builders.* They pay attention to developing a wide network of useful contacts, who can provide information and help. They also take care to keep their network in a good state of repair by doing small favours. Others, who may include some of the network builders, are *politicians.* They consider who needs to be influenced, and the methods that should be used to do so. They see relationships in terms of power, that is, their ability to influence others, and they do all they can to ensure that they are in as good a position as possible to do so. For some of those whom we studied it seemed to be an enjoyable game in which one exercised one's skill, rather than a response to an unstable environment.

Where and when the choice exists

The choice exists in most managerial jobs, but there are some where there is little or no scope for boundary management, and a few where there is no need. In organizations with highly formalized communications there may be little opportunity for the informal contacts that are the usual way of trying to manage one's boundaries with other departments. One company, for example, imposed very strict lines of communication. Most communications outside meetings had to be in writing and to go through formal channels. Managers were also told whom they might contact in external groups so as to avoid any duplication. There are some jobs where there is little need for boundary management. This is true of many of those in financial accounting, where formal procedures, supported by statutory requirements, may give little opportunity for other departments to disturb the unit's work.

There are two broad reasons why managers may seek to manage their boundaries. One is preventive: to try to ensure that the work of the unit is not disturbed by the actions of others. It was in that sense that the service manager quoted at the start of this chapter was speaking. The other reason is more strategic: to try to create the conditions where new developments will be accepted, or where the manager can expect support in times of difficulty.

An unstable environment affecting the unit creates a need for boundary management. This instability may be within the organization and/or outside it. Boundary management is possible only where action can be taken to prevent or modify the instability; otherwise one can only fire-fight. An area manager in a travel firm, for example, described herself as operating in a crisis industry where little can be done, apart from some contingency planning, to cope with unpredictable strikes of air transport controllers, airline baggage handlers, hotel staff, and others who can interfere with the transport of passengers and their accommodation.

The operation of the manager's unit can be affected by changes in the inputs to it, either in the nature of the work to be done or in the resources available to do it. The manager may wish to protect the unit from disturbances to either, or to change what is available. In some jobs the most important choices for the unit's effectiveness will be seeking to influence the nature and timing of the resource inputs. In many production management jobs this is the most important boundary, as supplies in the right form, quantity and at the right time will be vital to smooth operation. In some services jobs there will be a choice to try to influence the kind of work that comes to the unit.

In some jobs the need for boundary management may be primarily at the output rather than the input end. This is true where the manager has to sell the output or wants to get takers for a changed output. Selling can be as important for providers of internal services as for those with external customers. The manager may also wish to change users' expectations of when the work will be done. The users of typing pools, for example, may be unhappily aware of the exercise of this choice.

An important area for choice in some jobs is in trying to influence the regulatory conditions that affect the unit. One example is negotiations with trade unions, where managers may have a choice in whether they leave these to the industrial relations department or seek to get involved themselves. In companies where annual targets are set for managers, there can be a very tense period while managers seek to ensure that the targets for their units are not too difficult to meet. Production management jobs offer choices in seeking to influence those who are concerned with regulating working conditions and safety.

Choices in boundary management may be limited by demands and will be limited by constraints. Where disturbances pose a major threat to the unit's work the manager may *have* to act; it will be a demand. Senior management's expectations about the circumstances in which their managers will act may also create demands. In some organizations there will be constraints upon the methods of communication and upon whom the manager can contact. In most organizations there will be constraints from policies, procedures, and customs, and from the manager's status compared with those whom he or she wants to influence.

The structure, policies and procedures of the organization will affect the opportunities and the need for managers to seek to protect their units from disturbance. Its climate will affect the methods that they use to do so. A badly organized company will increase the need for managers to pay attention to boundary management; so will one that operates in an unstable environment. An organization that has uncooperative relationships among managers will encourage them to protect their units at the expense of others. Organizations, therefore, will in part determine the need for boundary management and the methods that are used.

Examples of choices in boundary management

In our observation of two service managers with similar jobs in the same company we noticed marked differences in the importance that they attached to boundary management. One of them, from whom we quoted at the start, said:

Almost anybody can screw up the work of the department. It is important to know who can do so most easily. For me it is the clerks in the accounts department, who can make problems about the expenses of my area managers. So I have to make time to explain to them the reasons for an apparent discrepancy. The other main person who can cause us problems is the sales manager, because his people can make promises that will make servicing very difficult. They can exaggerate a machine's capabilities and its freedom from service needs. I have to try and stop this happening.

The other service manager was not concerned about influencing people in other departments, with one exception: the design of the computer systems that controlled much of their work. He took a keen interest in systems design and in proposing systems that were more suited to his particular needs.

Managers who pay attention to boundary management are likely to be active in trying to ensure that their units get the supplies and resources that they want. A broad difference is between managers who play by the book, and leave supplies to those whose job it is in the organization to deal with them, without trying to influence their allocation, and those who try to ensure that their unit gets preference. The latter may choose to establish personal relations with suppliers. They may do them favours, such as testing a new product, in the expectation that the supplier in return will try to ensure that they get supplies even in a time of shortage.

28

The provision of favours, whether of goods, actions, or merely pleasantries, as a way of managing one's boundary is a method that is well understood by some managers. Anthropologists have shown that in many cultures the exchange of gifts is a common way of handling delicate relations. Some managers make use of such exchanges consciously or instinctively, but others have a more formal approach. They expect that the system will provide, or that a straightforward request is all that is necessary. The difference was commented upon by one production superintendent:

I suppose I like talking to people and I can usually get people to do things; an example is our Planning Office. I walked in behind someone who said, 'Could you do this and this on this date?' 'No', they said. I walked up and said to the same chap, 'Did you go down and see the City play on Saturday?' and we'd get chatting away, and I'd say, 'Could you do this for me?' 'Yes', he says and he'll do it. . . . You can get people to react if you get them off the subject and make them feel a bit relaxed and then sort of slip the question in and get the right answer.

There are many other ways by which managers can try to improve relations with those whose attitudes are important for the work of their units. There was the national sales manager who introduced what he called a 'fairy godmother scheme' to establish closer relations with production. Each sales manager was asked to develop relations with a particular factory manager and to address meetings at all levels in the factory to explain the needs of the market and the current market situation. There was the works manager who ran an annual open day for schools and parents to establish goodwill in the community and to attract good school-leavers. There are managers who make a point of getting to know local notables who might be in a position to provide useful support if there are problems in the community, or if there is a recession.

Implications

Ideally, an organization will want its mangers to be alert to the need to protect their units, and to create cooperative relationships for changes, but not to put the importance of doing so above the general good of the organization. The more alert that managers are to the choices that exist for boundary protection, the greater may be the danger that they will use these choices in a way that is suboptimal for the organization. Despite this danger, it seems desirable that more managers should be aware of the importance of boundary management and of the relevance of network-building to achieve it. Managers with a scientific background are likely, in our experience, to be most in need of help in understanding the importance of boundary management and the value of deliberately seeking to create cooperative relationships with other departments.

Boundary management is an important choice for the individual to consider when reviewing what he or she ought personally to be doing. It may be desirable to delegate much of the work within the manager's unit, but boundary management is a task that managers should often undertake themselves because they can make effective use of their position. Some managers focus too much of their attention upon their subordinates and are not sufficiently aware of the need for boundary management. It is worth checking whether that applies to you. First, compare the time that you are spending with your subordinates with the time you spend with others who are able to affect the work in your unit. Then, list all the people who are able to constrain or disturb what is done. Next, consider which of these you try to influence and what other opportunities for influence may exist. Boundary management is an area where managers can benefit from having clear objectives and a strategy and tactics for achieving them. The examples provide a few simple illustrations of these. In our experience, the suggestion that managers have found useful is that of paying more attention to building up and maintaining a network of useful contacts.

Summary

Boundary management entails trying to ensure that the operations of the unit for which one is responsible are not disrupted by the actions of those outside it, nor that new developments are hindered. Taking action to prevent such disruption is a choice that exists in most managerial jobs.

Managers differ markedly in their recognition of the existence of this choice and of the need to exercise it. The distribution of the manager's time between subordinates on the one hand and peers and seniors on the other is a crude guide to whether the choice is being used.

A common method of boundary management is to build up a network of friendly and useful contacts by the exchange of favours and pleasantries. Other methods are planning, and political calculations of who needs to be influenced and how to do so.

The need for boundary management will be influenced by the structure and climate of the organization and the relative instability of the unit's environment. In some units managing the nature and timing of inputs will be most important; in others it may be the acceptance of outputs or the regulatory conditions that an active manager will most wish to influence.

Boundary management is a task that managers should often do themselves, because their subordinates will usually be in a weaker position to do so.

4.
Choices of domain:
I. For one's unit

One can pick things up and run with them.

Engineering manager

The job has a very wide remit to provide computer services to the division. How he uses this remit will determine the job boundaries.

Boss of data processing manager

It is a job with very broad parameters. He was not told how to do it, or exactly what we wanted him to do, but just to recommend how we should develop our business in India.

Boss of business planning manager

The choice depends on whether he sees himself as an historian or as someone who participates in running the business.

Boss of controller

If he is a look-alive fellow he can make a real contribution to the business.

Boss of management accountant

What should my unit be doing? How should it be developing? Such questions would make no sense in jobs responsible for a clearly delimited area of operation. In the jobs that we shall consider in this chapter the manager has some choice to determine, or to try and change, what is done. Most of the jobs that we shall discuss are in charge of 'units', which is the general term used to cover such varied responsibilities as a department, section, division, store, branch, region, company, farm, laboratory, hospital, institute, and school. We shall also include jobs at the management level that have no responsibilities for staff, where the unit is just the individual who has a choice in deciding what should be done within the assigned responsibilities. Such jobs include short-term projects like the study, which was quoted above, of potential developments in India. The word 'domain' is used for the unit's area of operation.

An understanding of which jobs offer a choice of unit domain is important for selection, training, and development. Such jobs provide opportunities for strategic thinking. This is relevant to selection because many individuals who become managers are happier dealing with the concrete, with the on-going solution of problems, rather than with the longer-term thinking that is needed for developing a strategy. An understanding of these jobs is relevant to training because individuals in them can be helped to think in terms of strategies and of how to appraise their value. A choice of domain is also relevant to career development, as a sequence of jobs that require no strategic thinking is poor preparation for more senior posts.

Where and when this choice exists

Some choice of unit domain exists wherever the output is not clearly prescribed. Most top management jobs offer this choice, but it can also be found in many middle and even some junior management posts. It exists most commonly in staff and service jobs, in sales jobs that are not too constrained in their products and markets, and in posts heading up separate units, such as a branch or store, where the domain is not precisely laid down by head office; but some choice of unit domain can also exist in other kinds of jobs.

Many staff jobs have potentially flexible domains. The opportunity often exists to extend the areas in which information is provided or the services that are given. Many advisory jobs are flexible because their nature will depend in part upon the interpretation that the jobholder puts upon them. They can range from a very wide remit, like that quoted earlier to act as the organization's scout in a particular area, to a much more limited one with specific tasks that must be done, but also with opportunities for developing new ones.

Many jobs whose product is information offer a choice in the nature of the output. It can be just providing data or offering advice, or going further and trying to persuade the recipients that the advice is right. In some jobs, such as product management, there will be a demand to provide advice as well as information, but advocacy, where the opportunity exists, is always a choice. It is the choice of moving from a posture of neutrality to a more personal involvement in the nature and value of the information being provided.

We found that managers are more likely to recognize this choice than the others that we describe. Usually it was the jobholder who told us about it, so we did not have to rely, as we did for recognizing some of the other choices, upon the boss's comments, our observations, or the enquiries of other managers in the small teaching groups that we asked to explore the choices of one member's job. The consciousness of choice may have come from a sense of the risk involved in being known to advocate a particular line of action. We are usually aware that we do not have to speak out, but are choosing to do so.

Limitations upon choices of unit domain

Choices of unit domain may, like other choices, be limited by demands and will be limited by constraints. The demands are most likely to affect the time and energy available for developing and pursuing new activities. Present problems may so absorb the manager that no attention is given to considering whether the output should be changed. Self-imposed demands, such as making tours of the works in the morning and afternoon, will also limit the time and attention that can be given to considering changes in activities. The production superintendent quoted in the previous chapter, who divided his time between short-, and medium-, and long-term work, is unusual. It is more common for junior and middle managers to be caught up in the business of day-to-day management.

A major constraint upon a change of unit domain may be others' unwillingness to accept the output. The users may have fixed ideas of what they want and accept nothing else. The successful exercise of a choice of unit domain will often mean selling the benefits of the change to potential users. A marketing manager trying to promote a new product or to sell an existing one to a different kind of customer will know that there is a need for selling. It may not be recognized by staff and service managers in other functions. They may expect the virtues of what they are offering to be self-evident.

Policies that define what goods can be produced and what services can be provided are common constraints in large organizations. It is only where output requirements are in such general terms as a profit target that the manager will be relatively free of such constraints—'relatively free', because the profit target and external conditions may also limit what goods can be produced.

The availability of resources will be a constraint on some kinds of changes. Where more or different resources are needed the manager may have to get permission to acquire them. The abilities, interests and attitudes of the manager's staff can also be a constraint on making changes in the unit's work. They may be unable or unwilling to carry out different work. Yet another constraint may be the attitudes of colleagues in other departments who may see the manager as an empire builder whose ambitions should be kept in check. The array of constraints that can apply will mean that in some situations the choice, even if its existence is recognized, may be treated as hypothetical rather than actual. In such situations it is likely to be only the very determined, ambitious or restless manager who will seek to make changes in the unit's domain.

Examples of choices in unit domain

Different kinds of jobs offer different possibilities for choice of the unit's domain. There are some jobs that have a broad remit, although they may also include some specific tasks. Such jobs can provide considerable choice in the kind of work that is undertaken. There are the jobs that have a well defined domain with specified outputs that also offer some scope for new developments. This is true of a wide variety of jobs. Then there are the choices in information jobs to advise and to advocate the value of one's advice, not just to provide information.

Choices within a broad remit

Corporate planning is an obvious example of a job with a broad remit so that jobholders must choose what kinds of work should be done by them and their staff. One corporate planning manager commented:

One of the more difficult things about managing this activity with a very small number of people is that if you set your mind to it you can think of hundreds of things that we could look at. It's a matter therefore of continuously choosing and, having chosen, then you've got to be careful you don't sort of take on more and more things so that you do a lot of things half cock and none of them properly. So I wouldn't particularly encourage my staff to expand their job boundaries because there are not enough hours in the day.

This is an example of the difficulties that can come from having too much choice in the work that the unit can do. Managers in such jobs may complain of the burden of choice.

Senior personnel jobs can offer a choice between widely different types of work. One senior personnel manager, for example, when asked what work he did that another person in his job might not do, cited the following:

– Developing manpower planning on which to base recruitment policies
– Doing creative work on pay structures and their impact on people
– Encouraging participation
– Initiating surveys of employee attitudes
– Acting as a change agent by getting involved in management relationships

This example shows some of the different work in which a personnel manager may get involved. Another way of looking at these choices is in terms of the roles that a personnel manager plays. There may be a choice to take on, emphasize, or neglect the following roles:

– Guardian of the company's personnel policies and procedures
– Friendly helper
– Expert on legislation affecting employees

34

- Initiator of new personnel policies
- Change agent
- and a number of others

The job of a safety manager who was in charge of five safety officers in a chemical works is a good example of the possibilities of choices of work that exist in many advisory jobs, including those that combine in their job responsibilities elements of control as well as advice. The demand aspects of this job were to try and ensure that safety regulations were applied, to meet the factory inspector, and to keep up to date with any changes in safety regulations, and in unionized plants to consult with shop stewards about implementation of safety regulations. The constraints included the hazards of the equipment and processes used and the attitudes of management and workers to adhering to safety regulations and to trying to prevent accidents. Many of the constraints offered the choice of trying to change them. There was also a choice in the methods used to try to do so.

Accidents may be caused by failures of hardware, systems, building design, and human behaviour. These varied possible causes provide a choice for a safety manager who is innovative to explore particular interests. A manager in this particular job who was interested in physical sciences could develop a knowledge of, say, microbiology, if it was becoming important in the company, and seek to understand its safety implications. One who was more behaviourally inclined could investigate particular behaviours that are related to accidents. The innovative choices that existed in this safety manager's job meant that one jobholder could spend some of the time on tasks that were quite different from that of another, who limited activities to enforcement and consultation. The importance of safety of some plants for the community outside offers other possible areas of choice in whom the safety manager meets, and in the emphasis that is given to community relations and community protection.

Choices of additions to specified output

A plant engineer is an example of the choice that exists in some staff and service jobs of moving from more routine work to new developments. The plant engineer may be able to expand the boundaries of the unit from doing straight repairs to more developmental work. The personnel manager may be able to move from administering existing systems to developing new ones or even trying to change the ways in which managers behave towards their staff. The job of a management accountant can provide opportunities for trying to introduce new methods of costing. Like many staff jobs, it can be treated as somewhat routine or as offering scope for creative innovations that extend the unit's domain. The final two quotations at the start of the chapter testify to the choices that exist in many management accounting jobs.

35

Some jobs offer entrepreneurial possibilities for initiating new business activities. The choice in many general management jobs is sufficiently well known not to need illustration. Service jobs where the department's services can be marketed outside the organization also offer this choice. There are some examples in data processing. It can also be true of more unexpected jobs. Warehouse management, for example, seems like a job with a clearly defined boundary offering no choice of unit domain. However, one warehouse manager studied had extended his unit's domain in two ways. One was by selling any vacant space to outside customers. His own company had a seasonal business, so that stocks in the warehouses varied and were partly predictable. He could know when there was likely to be spare capacity that could be sold. The other way in which the warehouse manager had enlarged his domain was by taking over the servicing of fork lift trucks that had previously been done by the engineering department. He was currently investigating whether to develop this as a service that could be sold to other firms. His boss supported him in such entrepreneurial interests. Had he had a boss who opposed them, he would have had the choice of trying to persuade him.

Engineering services management is another example of a job where one incumbent had an entrepreneurial view of its possibilities for expansion. He said:

In any service activity there are lots of jobs that need doing but which fall between stools. Certain managers regard them as an unnecessary appendage to their jobs as they'd really like to get on with the main stream work. If you are prepared to pick up all these bits, the people to whom they nominally belong are delighted, and you expand your own job.

Sometimes managers assert that: 'one manager's choice is another's constraint'. This can be true but is not necessarily so. The choices made by a boss may constrain a subordinate's choice of unit domain, or they may increase it. The same is true of choices by colleagues. Even the expansionist choices of the engineering services manager may have been seen by some colleagues as increasing their choices by giving them more time to devote to the work that interested them.

Even in some jobs with well-defined unit boundaries, like those of a factory manager or a retail chain store manager, there may be opportunities for slight changes in what the unit does. The manager may be able to develop a reputation at head office for being interested in testing new products and may be good at reporting the results. For the store manager who is particularly interested in merchandising, this provides an opportunity to have a newer and more varied selection of goods. For the factory manager it provides some diversion from the more routine aspects of the job and an opportunity to use one's technical interests.

Hotel managers have slightly more flexibility of domain than chain store managers. They may, depending upon the constraints imposed by head office policy, be able to try and influence the type of customers that are attracted, making a special feature of conferences or weddings, or establishing close links with the local tourist board or particular travel agents. They may seek to develop a reputation for one particular service. 'I attach great importance to having a good restaurant. The food is the thing that people remember best', said one hotel manager. This is a job where such entrepreneurial developments may well be encouraged by head office, as distinct from those like the engineering services manager or the warehouse manager, which individuals have seen and carved out for themselves.

Choices in information jobs

The choice of advice and advocacy that exists in some information jobs can be illustrated by an operational research manager who took the choices available in information jobs much further than most. He believed passionately in the contribution that the models that he and his staff developed could make to planning the business. He could have played the job quietly, developing models that he was asked for and even making suggestions for new models. Instead, he took the riskier and for him much more interesting and worthwhile approach of developing his own planning models and then mounting an intensive programme of lobbying, by individual and group discussions and by formal presentations, to show that they could do. He developed his unit's domain from one of providing tools for policy-making to trying to influence the policies that were made. He did this so vigorously that the basic model became a political issue with its supporters and detractors.

It is unusual, in our experience, for an information manager to have such a strong sense of mission. Somwhat more common is the cooler, more calculating, approach of the head of market research in a large company who described the choices in his job. He saw the demands as selecting data, explaining, and offering advice. There were, he said, choices in the kind of advice that he gave, particularly in whether it was cautious or controversial. It could be controversial because it was more speculative than the nature of the job demanded. It could also be controversial because it was acceptable to some top managers but not to others. Where he knew this to be so he had a choice of taking the political risk that might be involved. He had further political choices if he was keen to get his views across. He could decide whom he most needed to influence and what were the best ways of trying to do so.

Implications

The examples that we have given of different kinds of flexibility of unit domain have important implications for management selection and training, for career planning, and for job design. 'Important' because they raise questions about the kind of managers that the organization[1] wants. Would a man like the warehouse manager or the engineering services manager be welcome? Would the organization like a safety manager who had such a broad view of the possibilities of the job? Or would the organization be happier with a manager like the production superintendent who said: 'I know the boundaries of my job and am quite happy with them'? The organization can seek to encourage managers to take a wide view of the possibilities in their jobs; to recognize choices and to think strategically about them. Alternatively, it can define boundaries clearly and narrowly and emphasize the need to keep within them.

The kind of choices that individuals want to take is one factor that should be considered in selection. This is particularly necessary in information jobs, when the following questions could help in getting a good match between the individual and the organization: Does the organization want cautious, reliable people who can be trusted to produce reliable information in the areas requested? Or does it require people who are interested in exploring what information is needed? Does it want people who can take a radical look at accepted opinions and provide information that challenges them? Or does it prefer those who are no trouble and do not seek to influence line managers? Does it want people who take a balanced judicial view of information? Or would it like some, at least, who have a more personal, more idiosyncratic, approach? Will it tolerate, even reward if they prove good, those who seek to promote their ideas? There needs to be recognition that many information jobs offer the kinds of choice that are described in this chapter. The organization should know what choices it favours and should recruit the appropriate people, that is, those who will want to take the choices desired. But if it goes for the more adventurous, there needs to be a recognition that the more active and original person may be much harder to live with, and may not fit the climate of the organization.

Only a few managers, the research described in Chapter 8 suggests, think strategically about the work that can be done by their units. It is much more common to pitch in and do the job in the way that comes most naturally from one's previous experience. That may not matter in jobs where there are no choices to be made in the unit's output; but in jobs that offer such a choice managers who do not think strategically about what work their unit should be doing may miss some of the potential in the job: potential that could make for greater effectiveness and also be more enjoyable for the jobholder.

---

1. Here, and elsewhere in the book, the organization is treated as if it is an entity with wishes. This is untrue, but it is a convenient shorthand for the managers who have to take decisions about other managers and other jobs within the organization.

Summary

A job that offers choices in unit domain has some flexibility in the area of operation for which the manager is responsible. This means that the manager can make some changes in the nature of the unit's output. Such choices commonly exist in top management jobs, but they are also found in some junior and many middle management posts, especially those in staff and services.

The choice may come from a wide potential domain from which the jobholder has to select what should be done. Examples are corporate planning and senior personnel jobs. In some jobs there are entrepreneurial possibilities of extending the activities of the unit. Jobs providing a routine service may be capable of expanding to include new developments. Even in the more clearly bounded jobs, one may be able to have some non-standard output by developing a reputation for being interested in new developments and good at testing them. Information jobs may offer a choice of providing not only information, but also advice, and of advocating the value of one's advice.

Jobs that offer choices of unit domain require a capacity for strategic thinking about what should be done. The greater the choice, the more important is such thinking for effectiveness.

5.

Choices of domain:
II. Outside one's unit

One can either do a routine job, just day-to-day management of 20 people, or be part of the overall management of the business. You can push out your sensory whiskers and know what's going on. There is almost limitless opportunity to get yourself contact with customers and with production.

Laboratory manager

I can be the man who knows about hospitals and who visits them, or a theoretical planning chap.

District administrator in the UK National Health Service

What is it important for me to do? This question is one that an effective manager needs to ask in many jobs; in a few, what needs doing is so clear that the question is redundant. In the previous chapter we considered one of the major choices that a manager may have in deciding what to do. It is whether any changes should be made in what the unit does, which we called the unit's domain. In this chapter we look at those jobs where managers have a choice of activities outside the unit for which they are responsible, which we shall call the manager's personal domain. In such jobs the question, 'what ought *I* to do?' can be of prime importance, especially where there is a wide variety of possible activities. Is there an unfulfilled need for someone to represent the organization outside? Should I try and change the attitudes of my colleagues to industrial relations? Ought I to help X sort out the problems of his department? One of the line managers needs to really understand what the computer can do for us, instead of leaving it to the specialists. Am I the most suitable line manager to do that? Should I seek to persuade our competitors that the only hope for the industry is to work together to increase our market? How important is it for me to spend time lobbying for business interests? Should I use my experience to act as a consultant in another part of the organization? Can I get my professional association better organized and more up-to-date? Is it justifiable for me to give some of my working time for charities or for public service? Should I find time to make contacts in schools and universities so that we get good recruits? Do I want to be known as the person who gives wise counsel and who is prepared to listen to people's problems? These are but some of the possibilities that may exist in jobs that have a very flexible domain.

Where and when this choice exists

The first and most common kind of choice of personal domain is that of *wider involvement in the organization* beyond the requirements of one's own unit. One aspect of this, the sharing of work with one's colleagues and boss, is a sufficiently distinctive characteristic of some jobs to be considered in a separate chapter. The second type of choice of personal domain is a more individualistic one, that of *becoming an expert.* This is also a distinctive enough choice to merit a separate chapter. The third kind of choice of personal domain is that of *taking part in activities outside the organization.* This is a large category covering many different kinds of activities.

A management team that meets regularly will usually offer the most common opportunities for managers to take an interest in and to get involved in problems beyond their own units. The quotation above from the laboratory manager shows that some jobs offer other choices to extend one's personal domain by taking a wider interest in the work of the organization

The opportunity to develop a personal domain can be seen as a choice to invite work or to do one kind of work rather than another. Some managerial jobs are so closely defined that there may be little or no opportunity to avoid work, other than by delegation; but in most there are opportunities to invite it by taking an interest in something outside the prescribed tasks. The retail chain store manager can, for example, take an interest in the retail market in the area. In large organizations one can become known as a good person to be on a working party or to take part in recruitment. Often there is work to be done that no one else is doing, so that an expansion of personal domain does not have to be at the expense of someone else's domain.

The potential choices of personal domain are very wide in some jobs, but the individual manager still has to have the time and the interest to make use of them. An essential for managers to be able to develop personal domains is to inherit, acquire, or develop competent and well-motivated subordinates. Another essential is that the pressure of demands in terms of the time and energy that they absorb is not too great.

The company, for example, that is run by frequent meetings will make more demands on the time of its managers than one that is not. The more senior the manager, the more time may be spent in meetings. In such companies senior managers may have a wider potential domain than their juniors but less time free from demands for cultivating it. However, as we shall see in Chapter 6, the meetings themselves may provide various choices of domain.

42

Organizational differences

Organizations differ markedly, our research found, in the extent to which they provide opportunities for managers to develop a personal domain. Such opportunities can be both external and internal. In some large companies there may be general personnel tasks that any manager can take part in, such as serving on job assessment panels, taking part in training, and university recruiting. There may also be a variety of other cross-functional tasks in which one can participate if one shows an interest, such as serving on working parties. In other companies there may be few or no such opportunities, and even where they exist it may be easier for a boss to object, saying 'It's not what he (or she) is paid for.'

There are also, we found, major differences between organizations in the extent to which they permit, or even encourage, their managers to do work outside the organization. Some organizations need more contact than others with a wide range of people outside, whether they are competitors, local councillors, educationists, the media, or any of the other groups whose activities and attitudes may be important for the organization. Organizations vary, too, in whether such outside contacts are made only the responsibility of particular individuals or whether there is general encouragement for managers to take part in external activities if they are interested. The organization's policies or customs about public activities can be a major constraint upon, or facilitator of, a choice of external domains.

The variations that we found in opportunities for personal domains in different organizations could not be explained only by differences in size or technology; nor, so far as we could tell, by other differences in the situation of the organization. Rather, they seemed due, wholly or partly, to differences in management philosophy. In one large organization that we studied there were opportunities for all managers to do some work other than that directly concerned with their own units, both within the organization and also usually outside it. In this organization it was expected that managers would both do their own jobs and, if they had time and were interested, share in the other tasks that needed to be done. Occasionally these expectations became demands rather than choices, but usually it was up to an individual to show an interest or to plead pressure of work if asked to do something outside the job's responsibilities. It was considered better in this organization to share such tasks rather than to assign them to particular specialists because it gave managers a better understanding of the organization and, externally, meant that the corporation both contributed to the community and established good relations with it. In another large organization in a highly technical industry managers were expected to confine themselves to the task for which they were paid. There was an exception: they could become experts, a form of personal domain that is discussed in Chapter 7.

Examples of choices of personal domain

Oportunities to get involved in the work of the organization outside one's own function exist in many top management posts, but they can also be found in jobs in middle and junior management. Some jobs naturally provide such an opportunity; management services is a good example, because a manager who is interested in developing improved models and programmes for management information must necessarily learn about the relevant aspects of the organization. Opportunities can also exist in less obvious jobs. The quotation from the laboratory manager at the start of the chapter is one such example. This particular manager saw the choices as:

to opt for a very quiet and dull life [or] . . . know what's going on, making contact with production and with customers. There is almost limitless opportunity to push back through those routes. The main choice is what you set as your limits, as your sphere of influence in the company, whether you want to be part of the overall management of the company.

He worked for a medium-sized subsidiary company. In a large company choices might be much more constrained, but there may be other opportunities, such as taking part in job evaluation panels or graduate recruiting.

One of the research studies on which this book is based provides a good example of a job offering a very wide choice of personal domain, both within the organization and outside it. It is that of district administrator in the National Health Service in the UK, which is a senior management post. Even though it is an unusual job, it can be used as an example because many of the domain choices that it offers exist in senior management jobs in other kinds of organizations. Our research provided a rare opportunity to study the work that was done and the methods used by a large number of senior managers in similar jobs. We studied 41, a fifth of all those in this job, selected to represent different district characteristics. Our brief was to describe what the job was really like and then to identify the training needs for it. We used the framework of demands, constraints, and choices to understand the job. We compared the similarities in what the administrators did, which we described as the demands, and the differences which, except where there were special local demands and constraints, represented the choices in the job. Our methods were lengthy interviews about the previous month's activities, records of contacts and meetings attended, and observations. The methods used are discussed in Appendix 1.

The district administrator is responsible for the administrative services in the health district. He is also a member of the district management team, which is responsible, within the resource and other constraints imposed by higher levels in the National Health Service, for health services in the district. A district can have a population ranging from about 100 000 to over

500 000. The district management team does not have a formal leader, and can choose whether to appoint a chairman and, if it decides to do so (which some of them did not), who it will be and for how long he or she will serve.

There was a wide variation in the size and nature of the domain that the district administrators occupied. The smallest domain was that of responsibility for the administrative services, which included acting as secretary to the district management team. Administrators occupying the smallest domain spent much of their time with their subordinates helping them sort out operational demands, and also responding to personal requests for information and help from doctors and other members of staff. Their role in the management team was predominantly secretarial and as spokesman for the administrative function. The largest domain was that of those administrators who felt themselves to be responsible for anything that happened in their district, and therefore sought to monitor the service that was being provided in it, and to influence those who they thought were not performing well. They attempted to lead as if they were the general manager, though the methods that they could use with doctors and nurses necessarily had to rely on persuasion and political sensitivity.

Most of the administrators occupied domains that were between the smallest and the largest possibilities. Within these two extremes there was considerable variation in which domains were the major focus of effort and which were not included in their attempts at influence. One major difference was between those administrators—the majority—who sought to lead their subordinates, and those who delegated this task to one or two senior subordinates. Those who delegated the leadership of their subordinates saw their major responsibility as lying elsewhere. Most frequently this was in seeking to guide the district management team: to set objectives, to try and ensure that the problems that mattered in the district were discussed and that agreement was reached on what should be done about them, and then in trying to ensure that such agreements were implemented.

One choice of domain was the activities that district administrators took on for the management team. They could speak on its behalf, either alone or with a colleague, at meetings of the lay authority. The choice here would be subject to various constraints including the wishes of colleagues. They could choose to be active in seeking to influence those who could affect decisions about the resources allocated to the district. They could be not merely the spokesman for the district, but also an advocate and lobbyist. They could choose to act as the figurehead for the organization, the person who was well known. One of the administrators we studied was called 'Mr Health' by the local newspapers.

There were yet other choices of domain, which are also common to many other management jobs. There was a choice to become active in professional associations; to take on responsibilities in the association; to be known as a person who could speak for the profession. There was a choice, too, in

45

establishing contacts with local universities, both to attract good students and to develop a network of people that might provide useful advice on some problems.

Indeed, the variety of possible domains open to the administrators, within the constraints of their own abilities, the expectations of the other members of the team, and the demands made by special difficulties in the district, meant that administrators could, and did, spend their time in very different ways. A description of the job that did not take account of the very different work that *could* be done would be far from describing its reality.

The job of the district administrator is also an example of the differences in constraints that can limit the choices even in similar jobs. These varied with the severity of the problems in the district, with inherited local attitudes to the hospitals, with the ability to attract good medical and nursing staff, with the expectations of the administrator's behaviour inherited from a previous incumbent, and with the personalities and attitudes of the leading doctors and the other members of the district management team. The latter will include the roles that they want to play. In a consensus management team there is even more scope than in the normal management team with an appointed head for individuals to play, and sometimes to compete for, different roles. The district administrator's choice, for example, to act as if he or she was the general manager or to play the figurehead may be constrained by the wish of another, and more dominant, member of the team to do so.

Kotter and Lawrence (1974), in a study of a very different kind of job, that of American mayors, described the domain as the different areas of city life in which the mayor sought to have an impact. There are parallels to the job of the district administrator even though one is an elected position and the other an appointed one. In both there is a wide choice as to what the individual can do. Both studies identified a number of radically different ways of doing the job. Both mayors and district administrators are particularly dependent, for their success in achieving their objectives, on their ability to influence people, since in many of their relations they are in a position of potential influence rather than of authority. The mayor is more dependent than the district administrator upon a capacity to develop a useful network of supporters, and on enlisting the support of at least some of the major influence groups in the city. The district administrator, like others working for a large organization, will have more ready-made contacts. The constraints that limit the mayor's choice are likely to vary more from one city to another depending upon his or her political position, the strength of different pressure groups, and the finances of the city, than will the constraints in different health service districts where membership of a large bureaucracy ensures somewhat greater uniformity.

An American mayor or a British district administrator in the National Health Service will not seem relevant to the manager in industry or commerce who takes a narrow view of what examples of managerial work are of interest to him. This would be mistaken, as both posts illustrate choices of domain that are found in many senior and some middle management jobs in companies.

Implications

It may be asked whether a job with a very flexible domain is a necessary one. There is no clear-cut answer, because one cannot point convincingly to a set of duties that merit the existence of a job and that must be performed by the jobholder when individual jobholders can spend their time in very different ways. It may be useful in such jobs to think of what should be done by a group of people rather than by only one person, which is why the next chapter will be on work-sharing.

One solution to the problem posed in the previous paragraph is to say that no job should be as flexible as that. Jobs that offer a wide choice of personal domain are anathema to those who favour clearly defined and delimited responsibilities. They will describe such jobs as a sign of poor organization, which will necessarily contribute towards ineffective management. We noted earlier that we found that organizations differed markedly in whether, and if so in the extent to which, they permitted or encouraged their managers to do work that was not directly relevant to their own units. We noted also that these differences could not be explained only by differences in technology.

There are obvious dangers as well as advantages for the organization in jobs that offer a wide choice of domain. The potential advantages are managers with a broader viewpoint and greater opportunities for self-actualization, as well as a wider representation in the community. The disadvantages are that managers may not give enough attention to their own units (though if they have competent subordinates this may not matter), and that the individual choices may leave gaps in what needs doing. The danger is that managers will pursue their own interests and inclinations without paying adequate attention to organizational needs, or to what they are best able to contribute. Managers who are in jobs that offer a choice of personal domain need, if they are to be most effective, a clear view of their objectives and of those pursued in practice by their colleagues. Such analytical and strategic thinking does not come naturally to many managers. Further, the total immersion in activity that the managerial environment so easily provides can make it difficult, sometimes even impossible, to do such thinking during working hours. Our research suggests that managers in jobs with flexible domains may need a stimulus, and an opportunity, to reflect on what most needs doing, and on whether their current choices of domain are the most appropriate.

There are two periods in a job when it can be especially useful for managers in flexible jobs to review the choices of personal domain offered by the job. One is when they are newly appointed, and should try to take an overview of the possibilities. The other is when they have been in the job for some time and have exhausted the possibilities that they recognized. Then is the time to consider what other domains may be available. The identification of new domains that can usefully be exploited can help to provide a renewed interest in a job that may otherwise come to be seen as too familiar and therefore dull.

Some individuals may develop domains outside the organization because they are out of sympathy with its climate, and may use external contacts and activities as a way of escaping. Rapoport (1970, pp. 241–2), in a study of the careers of managers who had been through a senior executive programme at the Administrative Staff College at Henley, distinguished this as a career pattern that he called 'tangential'. He commented on the benefits to their organization that could come from this:

As the environment changes and the internal structure evolves in a way only partly geared to these changes, situations often arise in which there is a shift of emphasis and the individuals working on the periphery become of central importance to the enterprise. A marginal activity is always worth monitoring as a potential new frontier, and managers with this source of proclivity are therefore worth cultivating as potential leaders if a new direction is struck.

Summary

Many jobs offer a choice of different kinds of work outside the manager's unit. There are three broad possibilities: getting involved in other aspects of the organization's work; becoming an expert; and taking part in activities outside the organization. These are the personal domains as compared with the unit's domain.

The opportunity to develop a personal domain can be seen as a choice to invite work or to substitute one kind of work for another. In many jobs there are opportunities to take an interest in something outside the prescribed tasks. However, how much and what kind of choice there is will depend both on the nature of job and upon the policies and customs of the organization. There are wide organizational differences in the opportunities to pursue personal domains both inside and outside the organization.

The potential choices of personal domain are very wide in some jobs—so wide that jobholders can spend a majority of their time doing quite different kinds of work. In such jobs the manager should ask: 'What is it most important for me to do?' The answer should depend, in part (as we shall see in the next chapter), upon what others are doing.

6.
Work-sharing

I have developed an interest in finance so that I work closely with the controller on the costing of new projects.

Production director in an engineering company

Whichever of us is in the office will deal with customers' queries.

Marketing manager

Two or three of us will represent the team on some hospital visits.

District administrator in the UK National Health Service talking about the management team

So far we have talked about jobs as single entities, even though recognizing that the opportunities for choice that they provide are limited by the demands and constraints that come from other people. In some jobs there is a greater need to consider the related posts because work may be shared between them. The range of choice offered by such jobs is increased because the work that is done by different people will be somewhat fluid. This is true for posts like the senior administrators who were the subject of our fourth study, for members of some management teams, and for posts with deputies. Job descriptions, selection, and training ought to take such work-sharing into account, and any realistic appraisal of effectiveness must do so.

Work-sharing may be upwards, downwards, or sideways. We shall mainly discuss sideways sharing, but we should recognize that the term can also be appropriately used between boss and subordinate(s). Sideways sharing can mean flexibility in what work is done, and by whom, at the boundaries between jobs. It can entail one manager getting involved in work that is part of the core of another's job, such as sharing in tackling some major problem. It can also mean two or more managers jointly choosing to get involved in work that concerns the team as a whole.

Work-sharing is recognized in classical writing in two respects: delegation

49

and staff jobs. In both it is expected that there should be a clear division of work and of responsibility. Delegation is acceptable to upholders of organizational clarity because the manager retains accountability and can allocate responsibility to those to whom work is delegated. But this presents a rather static, formal picture of work and its division. In some situations the manager and immediate subordinate(s) may work as a team with a freer and changing division of work in response to the pressure of events.

Work-sharing may be seen as running counter to individual accountability. It is all right, it may be argued by the classically minded, provided it is still clear who is responsible for what. In some examples of work-sharing this can be true, but in others it becomes more diffuse. Accountability is fully possible only where there is exposure, because mistakes or poor performance are clearly the responsibility of the individual. It seems likely that the more complex the organization and the more senior the job, the less exposure there may be, because of the diverse involvement in decision-making and sometimes even the difficulty of tracing when a decision was taken. Stewart (1976) suggested the concept of exposure and showed how this differed between jobs.

Where and when the choice exists

Work-sharing can take place between boss and subordinates, where there is no clear difference of knowledge and skill between them and no rigid status differentiation between levels. The senior may choose to work as a member of a team and share work fluidly, as did some of the administrators whom we studied. Such fluid sharing may also come, as in some marketing jobs, from frequent absences abroad, so that whoever is in the home office must cope with the work that comes in. Managers with deputies are more likely to follow a fairly regular pattern, with one person tending to do particular kinds of work. One person may, for instance, manage the unit while the other is the front man for outside contacts. Such a division of work may result from delegation or from a gradual adaptation to individual interests.

There are two different kinds of work-sharing among members of management teams, both of which can offer opportunities for choice. The first is the different roles that are played in groups. Studies of small group behaviour have taught us a lot about these. They have shown, for example, that there tend to be task leaders and social leaders (Bales, 1950). A more elaborate version of the analysis of different roles was provided by Belbin, Aston and Mottram (1976), who identified eight different roles that can be played in a management team. These include Resource Investigator, who goes outside the group and brings back information and ideas to it, and Monitor Evaluator, who contributes a measured and dispassionate analysis. These roles included the idea of choice, as Belbin and his associates argued that individuals would have a preferred role, but might be capable of playing another. Groups, they suggested, could benefit by analysing their behaviour and seeing what roles were not being performed and whether any of their number might be able to take them on. There will be some variation in the roles needed according to the tasks of the group.

Membership of different management groups is a characteristic of matrix organizations and other complex structures. Such membership can provide different opportunities for choice because the composition of the group will vary, and so may the contenders for different roles. An individual may have the opportunity to play a particular role in one group that is taken by a more powerful contender in another group.

The second form of work-sharing within a management team has received less attention than group roles. It is the sharing of certain tasks between two or more members as well as the flexible performance of tasks on behalf of the group. The first kind of work-sharing—the adoption of group roles—applies in any group: the second does not. Only some management teams work fluidly so that the tasks performed by members are not limited to those that belong to the specific position. There are even top management groups where the sharing is more fluid than that, because some members do not have specific functions.

The nature and the opportunities for sharing of tasks between two or more colleagues will depend in part upon the knowledge and experience that each can contribute to the other(s), the need for such knowledge, and the existence and recognition of common problems. There are some opportunities for work-sharing between certain line and staff jobs, such as a general manager and a controller, or production and engineering managers. In such pairs each needs the knowledge possessed by the other. Each will also have some choice in the extent to which they confine their activities to their own function, take an interest in that of the other, and involve themselves in the broader problems of the organization. How much choice there is for such work-sharing will vary with the policies and climate of the organization.

In jobs where sideways work-sharing is possible there are two constraints that may inhibit it. The first is the pressure of other work. This is one reason why sideways work-sharing is probably found more commonly at senior levels, where the detailed management of operations can be delegated and the manager is freer to look sideways rather than downwards. The second is the attitude of other people to such sharing. The attitude of bosses can be a constraint if they have clear views about job responsibilities that do not include work-sharing. The major constraint is likely to be the attitude of the other person. He or she may be so absorbed in his or her own work as to have no inclination either to take part in work for the organization as a whole, or to help with problems of the other person's job. There may be a different kind of constraint, which comes from a resentment of what is seen as territorial invasion when one manager wants to get involved in the work of another.

Examples of work-sharing

The main example of work-sharing comes from the study of the district administrator in the National Health Service, because the extent and variety of work-sharing was one of the striking characteristics of this job. This post was described in the examples in Chapter 5, to which readers are referred for the background information. It provides a good example because we found parallels in top management groups in companies.

There is a major choice for individuals in the district management team as to how far they focus on the work of their own function and how far they involve themselves in the work of the team as a whole and/or of individual members of it. There is a choice in the interest they take, or do not take, in the organization's problems; in the work they do on behalf of the organization rather than just their own function; and in work-sharing with individual members. In the district management team there is also a more unusual choice of representing the team on visits and at meetings. In other groups the latter choice may exist only where the leader of the group does not monopolize such activities.

There are a number of roles to be performed on behalf of the district management team, some of which are demands and many of which are choices. These include visits by team members to hospitals, where they go as members of the team to look at conditions and problems, as distinct from visits that they may make on behalf of their own function. There is contact with local bodies, whose attitudes can affect the work of the team. There are the meetings of the governing body. In all these there is a choice for the team as to how far they attend meetings collectively, or at least with several members of the team, and how far they agree that one of their number shall represent them. The team can also decide whether it wants to undertake certain tasks, and if so how the work is to be shared. The individual has a choice of showing a willingness or a reluctance to undertake these representational tasks.

Diffe. ent jobs in the district management team, as in other management teams, offer various choices in work-sharing. The district administrator, together with the finance officer, offer the most choice because their information and knowledge is of the widest currency. This gives them a greater opportunity to contribute to the jobs of the other members. However, the opportunities that the administrator has for work-sharing also vary according to the nature of the other jobs in the team. The job in which the district administrator most commonly got involved was that of the district nursing officer.

The opportunity for work-sharing in the district management team that provides the best parallel with other types of organization was that between the administrator and the finance officer. The administrators varied considerably in the extent to which they took an interest in financial issues outside their own departments. They could choose, and some did, to work closely with the finance officer on developing financial plans for the district. They could also choose to support the finance officer's emphasis on costs or to side with what tended to be the medical and nursing view that high standards of patient care were more important than punctilious attention to budgetary controls. Supporting the finance officer could mean working together to develop a plan for action and spending time on trying to enlist support for it from other team members.

Some posts, like that of an accountant, will naturally provide knowledge that is of common currency. In others, the manager may have to acquire the relevant knowledge before he or she can share in work either with the team or with an individual member. This was true for the buildings superintendent, who was a member of the chief officer's team in a local authority. He had taken the time to acquire the necessary information about planning, and to read committee papers carefully so that he could contribute fully to discussions.

There may be opportunities to acquire an expertise that is of common currency and thus open up choices for work-sharing. The most common example is management services, especially in smaller organizations, where one member of a management team may acquire knowledge and take on responsibility for work in management services. Among the examples of this that we saw was the technical manager in the top management group of a medium-sized engineering subsidiary, who took an interest in the development of computer services and used this knowledge to work with two of his colleagues on the development of applications to their departments.

There are a number of reasons why managers may seek to get involved in the work of a colleague's department. One is a concern for the effectiveness of the organization as a whole and a feeling that a particular colleague is in need of help; this was one of the reasons given by the administrators who got involved in nursing problems. Another is to try and overcome some problems that that department may cause for their own departments. Choices exercised for these reasons may be deplored by the individual as costly in time and effort that might be better spent elsewhere. There are other reasons for involvement that will be viewed positively by him or her if not by their colleagues. One is a search for pastures new, either because they are bored with their own department or they feel that it is now running well and they should turn their energies elsewhere. There may be another reason, which can overlap with any of the previous ones: the desire to exercise influence over a larger area.

Implications

The existence of work-sharing among managers can be looked at from two opposite points of view. One is the benefits that it can bring: the greater effectiveness that can result from making use of the different knowledge and talents so that strengths are exploited and weaknesses compensated for. This is one reason why some senior managers take others with them when they go to a new company; they may have built up a team whom they know work well together and complement each other. The contrary point of view is that work-sharing is a deplorable sign of lack of organizational clarity, leading to confusion of accountability, to the danger that someone may neglect his own responsibilities because he finds a colleague's area of work more attractive, and sometimes also to the difficulty of determining which jobs are really necessary. Both points of view can be valid, though one will be truer in a particular situation.

The implications for the organization are to take the existence of this type of choice into account in considering selection, appraisal, and training, and to try and avoid or limit the disadvantages that may stem from it. There is a need to review the jobs in which work-sharing is likely to be beneficial, as well as the situations in which the opportunities for such choice will exist. Sharing can be beneficial because the occupants are likely to have complementary knowledge and abilities, or because it is known that a particular individual has weaknesses that need to be offset. An example of the latter is the manager whose originality of thinking can offer a lot, but whose lack of political sensitivity may mean that the ideas are never likely to be accepted. Such an individual will be able to contribute more if teamed with somebody with the necessary political skills.

It is customary in many appointments to consider how the individual will fit with others. An argument of this chapter is that for some jobs this needs to include whether the individual's likely choices will complement those of the people with whom he or she should work most closely. These choices include both the role that is adopted and the kinds of work that are taken on. The need to consider these is more often recognized in the appointments of deputies than for members of management teams. The latter are usually seen as appointments to a particular function rather than as also part of a work-sharing team.

The leader of a management team should try to encourage fruitful work-sharing, where this is appropriate, and to discourage inappropriate movements into another's area of work. The latter should include checking any personal tendency to trespass into a subordinate's sphere of work. There is a temptation for senior managers promoted from work they enjoyed to use some part of a subordinate's job as a play area.

Attention could usefully be given in many management teams to the roles that are played by different members so as to identify any that are missing and that may be needed for the effective functioning of the group. Belbin (1981) provides a full discussion of a useful approach to doing this. An awareness of which roles individuals play can also help members to recognize more readily the effects of changes in group membership.

Work-sharing has implications for appraisals. It means that for some jobs appraisal of individuals' performances in their immediate responsibilities is not sufficient. An appraisal may also be needed of pairs who should work fruitfully together, which considers how far they do in practice complement each other. There should be an appraisal of how well the members of a top management team are working together to improve the performance of the organization as a whole and to prepare for the future.

For the individual manager, the recognition of the choices that exist in work-sharing can provide another perspective on one's job. It can help one to consider whether one is making a contribution where it is most needed. It should help one to review whether one is giving the right amount of attention to managing one's own unit, to helping individual colleagues, to using the aid that they can offer, and to working with others members of the management team on broader problems of the organization. One should check that one is not prone to the danger of the individualistically minded manager who operates as if neither colleagues nor even subordinates are a potential resource.

Work-sharing can also be viewed in terms of its effect on the distribution of power. We found that the district administrators we studied had one of four possible relationships with other officers on the management team. These were: independent, where they both operated as independently as possible; dependent, where one was dependent upon the other for help; counter-dependent, where the relationship was antagonistic and offers of involvement had been repulsed; and inter-dependent, where they worked together on common problems of the district. Which relationship was likely to contribute most to the effectiveness of the team as a whole varied with the particular jobs, the strengths and weaknesses of the individuals, and the problems facing the districts.

Some relationships may necessarily be dependent. As a production manager one is necessarily dependent upon a number of people other than one's subordinates to provide the materials and services that are needed. But some dependencies can be a choice, because one has turned to the other person for help or allowed him or her to become involved in the work of one's department. Such dependence gives the other person some power over one. This may not matter, but for the manager who thinks in terms of relative power it is something to be considered in asking for help, in accepting it, or in providing it.

Summary

Some jobs offer opportunities for sharing work with colleagues. Such sharing increases the choice of work. Work-sharing, rather than delegation, can also exist between boss and subordinates where the work is shared fluidly between them.

There are pair jobs that offer choices of work-sharing, such as plant manager and plant engineer or manager and deputy. In a management team two or more members may work together, particularly where the knowledge and experience of one can contribute to the other, or where both are concerned with future planning or with tackling a major problem. In the consensus teams studied in the UK National Health Service there are also choices in who represents the team.

Work-sharing has implications for accountability and for appraisals. Performance assessment in some jobs may need to be of the individual, of a pair, and of the team.

Individual managers in jobs with a choice of work-sharing should review whether they have the balance right between the attention given to managing their unit, to working with colleagues individually, and to working with other members of the management team on the wider problems of the organization. They should assess what contribution they can make, while recognizing that made by others.

7.

Becoming an expert

If you are interested in a job and show a particular expertise people will gravitate towards you.

Distribution manager

I feel tall when people from outside the department come to consult me.

Production superintendent

There's a very great deal of satisfaction when one is involved in something that is original, new, and when you can produce something that can be useful, that's a very strong motivation. You know I should hate to go to the grave feeling that I hadn't really left anything behind me.

Plant engineer

One of the distinctive opportunities for choice that is offered by a surprisingly wide range of jobs is that of becoming an expert. There are, of course, jobs where the provision of expertise is a function of the job. The choice that we shall consider here is that of developing an expertise beyond, or other than, that required of the jobholder. Often this will take the form of developing a special expertise in one aspect of the job, or using one's expertise for purposes other than those that are a demand of the job. This choice is one form of personal domain. It is treated separately to highlight its special character. It exists in some jobs that do not otherwise offer a choice of personal domain.

This choice is of interest because it needs different abilities from the others that we have discussed. They are more dependent for their realization upon the manager being able to persuade others to cooperate in the exercise of the choice. They may require, too, the ability to develop a network of supportive relationships. The development of expertise can be a more individualistic activity. It thus offers an opportunity for choice to a manager who may not have the skills for exploiting other distinctive choices in the job; the common choices described in Chapter 2 are available in all jobs and will be exercised by all jobholders.

This choice, like others, will be attractive to some managers and not to

57

others. Schein (1975) developed the idea of career anchors, which individuals develop and use as a guide to the kind of jobs that will suit them. One of these Schein described as technical/functional competence, which characterizes people who are mainly interested in the specialist content of the work that they are doing. The choice that we are considering here may be related to this career anchor but does not seem to be identical with it. Individuals may pursue the choices of expertise described in this chapter but still be interested in the managerial aspects of their jobs.

There are also, it seems, national as well as individual differences in the attractions of expertness. This has been investigated by Bass and his associates in a number of different countries (Bass et al., 1979). He asked managers to rank 11 life goals in order of importance. One of these is called 'expertness', defined as 'to become an authority on a special subject; to persevere to reach a hoped-for expert level of skill and accomplishment'. He found marked national differences in the relative importance of different life goals, including expertness. Twenty-nine per cent of the British managers ranked expertness among the top three in importance. This was lower than any other country except Italy, for which the figure was 22 per cent. For the United States it was 32 per cent. The highest was the Netherlands, at 50 per cent. This suggests that more Dutch managers will look for and enjoy the choice of developing expertise, and that those who are promoted beyond the specialist level may still seek to retain an area of expertise.

Where and when the choice exists

The availability of this choice is determined, our research suggests, by the kind of company as well as by the type of job. We found marked differences between companies in the existence of this choice, as we did for other choices of personal domain. The company with a complex and rapidly changing technology, or one with specialized markets, will offer more choices of expertise than one with simpler technology and markets. The extent to which the organization is what Burns and Stalker (1961) called 'organic' is probably the most important difference between companies in determining the availability of this choice. Organic organizations have informal communications that go across functions and levels. These make use of knowledge wherever it can be found, irrespective of hierarchy. In such organizations individuals are freer to develop expertise and their knowledge is more likely to be known and used.

Larger companies will usually offer more opportunities for choosing to develop expertise than smaller ones. In a smaller company managers will often have to have a broad knowledge about many aspects of their job. A large company has more use for specialized expertise. In a very large organization there may also be a chance of becoming a temporary expert by being the first person to make use of a new technology, such as mini computers.

A wide variety of jobs can offer this choice in a suitable company. There are the opportunities to become an expert in one aspect of a technical job, particularly where knowledge is changing. There are opportunities in many staff jobs, such as management accounting, to become particularly knowledgeable about some aspect of the job, such as inflation accounting, or methods of cost control that are new to the company. Many marketing jobs provide opportunities, beyond the requirements of the job, for becoming known in the company as the person to consult about a particular market. Personnel jobs can offer a wide variety of possible expertise, such as recent legislation, or the use of new techniques. Some expertise, like that of new personnel techniques, may be relatively short-term, since the fashion or the need for the knowledge may change; others may be built up over a long period and may even provide the basis for a new job.

The availability of this choice will vary even in companies of the same size and in similar businesses. The forms of communication and the expectations of senior management can act as a constraint. Senior managers may welcome and make use of the special expertise that individuals choose to develop, or they may think that their managers should concentrate upon the mainstream aspects of their jobs. An individual's boss's attitudes can be a major constraint, as for example the management services manager who said of the systems manager:

He could specialize in certain types of system and acquire a reputation for these within the company and outside, but I would not favour that. It is non-productive. His people are overloaded so he should not think about other activities. The priorities are clearly laid down. His people know exactly what they are supposed to do.

The pressure of work that must be done will limit and may prevent the choice of developing the special interests that can lead to expertise.

Examples of choices of expertise

The production superintendent in the electrical department of an aircraft manufacturer had spent many years in the same job. He developed a special interest in avionics, studying the subject and trying to understand how developments would affect the manufacture in future. He hoped that his knowledge of the subject would help to convince senior management of its importance and of the need to set up a special department for it with himself as the manager. A technical manager in the textile department of a retail chain store held a newly created post that had arisen from the interest that he took in new materials in his previous job. Both managers are examples of situations in which the development of special knowledge can lead to the creation of a new job, even a new department. Indeed, in some companies the establishment of a

59

new job may be traced to the particular knowledge and interest that the first jobholder had shown in an earlier position.

In the head office of one large electronics company as many as 50 members of the staff were known for a particular expertise in addition to their official job. It had become customary in this rapidly changing technology for individuals to take an interest in some new development or particular market and to be known as the person to go to when one wanted information about it. Opportunities for developing expertise also exist in companies in less technical industries. In a travel company, which had very informal communications, individuals could develop special interests in particular markets or countries. One became known as the person to go to for information about planning tours in Finland; another for his special knowledge of skiing holidays. The latter was an area manager, not a marketing manager whose job it was to explore different types of holiday; but as he was a keen sportsman and excellent skier he could contribute his personal knowledge of what different resorts had to offer the accomplished skier.

A particular event can spark off an individual's interest in a subject. An accident in a chemical works stimulated one of the plant engineers to explore in depth the hazards of a particular process. For a few years he was the company's expert on the subject. A personnel manager in a large company who had a physically handicapped child had become very knowledgeable about the conditions in which certain types of physical handicap could be employed. She used this knowledge to advise personnel staff throughout the company about the recruitment and placement of physically handicapped people.

Some jobs, like that of the personnel manager and the area manager in the travel firm, can offer opportunities for an individual to use knowledge in the company that is developed outside, either in their private life, as in the two examples, or from previous training. Even very formalized organizations, where the content of jobs is clearly defined, may still make use of special expertise that is not a requirement of the job. This was true for a maintenance manager in a large local authority who had been trained as a civil engineer. It was because of this training and experience that he sat on an advisory committee for the city.

The examples so far have all been of how individuals were able to make use of previous knowledge or had developed an interest of their own accord that was not a demand of the job. Occasionally the opportunities for a choice of expertise are spelt out. This was true in the marketing department of a large company where marketing managers at a particular level were given the option of becoming an expert on a particular country or continent in addition to their product responsibilities. One of these managers had become the company's expert on Latin America because his work had frequently taken him there and he had become interested in the culture of the different countries he visited. He had learnt Spanish and Portuguese, and had established wide contacts in the industry there. This was a choice of expertise that was permitted only to managers at a particular level. However, the special interests that a manager developed in the level below could help him to exercise such a choice if he was promoted.

Implications

An organization that permits sufficient flexibility in jobs for individuals to pursue their own interests to the extent of developing expertise can gain two advantages. One is that the increased knowledge will be useful and may also lead to new developments, occasionally even to a new business or to new markets for existing business. The development of individual expertise may provide pointers to the directions in which the organization should be moving. Individuals, by their varied approaches, can supplement the more formal activities of future planning, and occasionally even of the research and development department.

The other advantage is that individuals will gain satisfaction from the opportunity of developing an interest of their own choice and from the recognition and use of their knowledge. It is a way in which an individual can get recognition and status without promotion. It can be a non-financial motivator. The danger, which those who think that individuals should spend their whole time on clearly defined tasks will be quick to point out, is that too much time and energy may be devoted to the pursuit of special interests rather than to the mainstream aspects of the job. No doubt this sometimes happens, but it was rarely mentioned by the bosses who described the opportunities in their subordinates' jobs for the development of expertise.

The example of the marketing managers at a particular level who could choose to specialize in a geographical area in addition to their product responsibilities may appeal to some as a good compromise between too little and too much opportunity for a choice of expertise. It may be a useful approach where one knows what kind of expertise would be useful, but can still leave the initiative to the individual to develop and get recognition for this choice. Even in more formalized companies where there is limited scope for uncharted change, such as retail chain stores, there may still be morale advantages, and occasional business spin-offs, from allowing some flexibility for the development of expertise.

Opportunities to develop expertise have advantages for the individual, though only some people will want to make use of them. There is the satisfaction that comes from pursuing a special interest. For a few this will be the main advantage, but many will also appreciate the recognition implied by people turning to one for information. It is a satisfaction that can be obtained without promotion, and which can offer an outlet for those who have been in the same job for a long time. Sometimes it can also provide an opportunity for using interests that one has acquired in one's private life. The development of expertise can be used to further, or to change, one's career by opening up new forms of work that one can do; sometimes even a newly created job, department, or even company. Expertise offers a choice that can suit the more individualistic manager because it is less dependent upon the cooperation of other people than many of the other choices; it therefore makes less demands upon social skills. For the more politically minded manager expertise can be used as something to trade against the cooperation of others.

Most managers who exercise the choice will probably do so without consciously selecting it; their interest will be aroused, and will develop as they pursue it. However, those who would like a change could help to achieve it by asking themselves: 'Where can I make a niche for myself that is not occupied by others?'

Summary

A surprisingly wide range of jobs offer a choice of developing an expertise beyond, or other than, that required of the jobholder. It is a choice that exists more commonly in organic and in large organizations. Even in these the extent of the choice will vary with the expectations of senior management and of the individual's boss, who may want total attention to the main task.

It is a more individualistic choice than the others that we have considered, hence it needs fewer social skills. The exercise of the choice can be beneficial to both the organization and the individual. The organization gets the extra knowledge, which may lead to new developments, even new business; it also gets a more motivated employee. The individual gets the satisfaction of pursuing a special interest and the recognition that it may receive. Occasionally, it can lead to new career possibilities.

PART TWO
The individual's view of the job

8.

How managers see choice

I suppose I must choose, but I never stop to think about it.

Engineering services manager

Things happen. Don't think about it. You do the job to the best of your ability.

Sales manager

I think that it is human nature to be more aware of the constraints than of the freedoms. You generally work within these constraints and are not really proactively, consciously aware of the freedoms you're exercising.

Works engineer

I try to operate as if there are no constraints. You may say that is impractical. But I find that I can look at a problem and think about the solution to it almost in isolation, and can get reasonably fixed in my mind whether or not it is a sensible idea. If it is, then I can sit back and say, right, that is what I aim to achieve: now what are the constraints that will stop me? Some I can deal with myself. Other constraints I may need to persuade superiors. I take the view that if you allow constraints to influence initial thinking you discard lots of possible propositions.

Production manager

So far we have talked about jobs and about the opportunities for choice that they offer. We gave examples of the choices that individual managers exercised, but that did not tell us how they thought about these choices, or even whether they thought about them at all. Our understanding of the implications of choice in managerial jobs will be incomplete unless we now turn from an analysis of jobs to an exploration of how managers themselves see opportunities for choice. The purpose of this chapter is to describe what the managers whom we studied, and those that we worked with on courses, said about their perceptions of choice.

The information for this chapter comes, in part, from two of the research projects—the third and fifth given in the table in Appendix 1—in both of which managers were asked about how the opportunities for choice in their present jobs compared with their previous ones. The fifth research project provides the main information as it was specifically about how managers see choice (Marshall and Stewart, 1981b). This study was limited to middle managers, mainly in production, technical, marketing, and sales jobs, in three manufacturing companies. Some of the tape-recorded answers to the questions asked are given above. The other source of information is from the many management courses where middle and senior managers from a wide variety of jobs and organizations were given the framework of demands, constraints, and choices and asked to examine, in small groups, one member's perceptions of his or her job in these terms. It is noteworthy that the other members of the group usually thought that the individual was overrating the demands and constraints and therefore underestimating the available choices.

Awareness of choice

The quotations above show that managers differ in whether they say that they are conscious of choice. A few were very aware of choosing, such as the production manager quoted at the start—he attributed his analytical thinking to having spent some time in a work study department. Most of the managers, both in the research interviews and on the courses, reported that they were normally unconscious of choosing what action they took, or what decision they made. They were carried along by the momentum of what happened, as the sales manager quoted above put it. Only occasionally were they aware of having to choose, for instance, when times of meetings clashed, or when something unusual happened that made them consider what they should do. However, though they said that they were not normally conscious of opportunities for choice, most of them could describe, when asked, some of the choice possibilities in their job.

The managers who said that they were conscious of choice gave different kinds of illustrations. Some had a mainly negative view; they described what they could choose not to do, or not to do then.

I frequently think of choice in the sense of looking at something and thinking: 'Sod that, can't be bothered with it today'.

Quite a number thought in terms of priorities:

I start off each day planning an agenda.

I divide work between the immediate, the current, tomorrow, and the future and try to make time for each.

Some commented upon a choice of style:

I think one fundamental choice is the basic style that you bring to bear on any job as a

66

manager; it's a question of whether you decide to lead from the front or from the back.

A few talked about choice in the longer-term aspects of their jobs:

On the long-term things I am very conscious of choice; I spend lots of hours mulling things over and thinking of what the long-term implications would be, and what the results would be if the decision were slightly different.

The difference between the majority of managers, who said that they normally did their job in their own way without being aware of making a choice, and the small minority, who described a more conscious, analytical approach to some aspects of their job cannot be explained solely by differences in their jobs. People in similar kinds of jobs also differed greatly in their awareness of choice. We do not know how far the explanations of these differences is one of personality and upbringing and how far it comes from later training and experience, but both have implications for management selection and training which we shall consider in Chapter 12.

What gives one choice

In the interviews and the course discussions managers described what factors they thought gave them opportunities for choice and what ones constrained them. Broadly, opportunities for choice were seen by most managers as existing when other people did not tell you what you should do. This 'freedom'—and that word was sometimes preferred to 'choice'—could come in a number of ways: from being given a larger job with more responsibility; from (and this was seen as very important) having one's own defined area of responsibility within which you were free to manage as you thought best: from having a new job so that you did not inherit the constraints of established ways of doing it; and from being an expert working for a boss who did not share your expertise. The freedom to do one's job in one's own way was considered important, both by managers who said that they were conscious of opportunities for choice and by those who said that they were not.

Managers were asked to describe in what ways their present jobs gave them more or fewer opportunities for choice than their previous ones. Their answers show what factors individual managers thought were important. Most were able to suggest differences, though sometimes only in general terms, such as:

Now I am a bigger fish in a smaller pond.

Hotel manager

I am less supervised, so can decide detailed objectives and priorities.

Production superintendent

67

The latter was a common answer of those managers who saw promotion as having given them more freedom to take their own decisions. Some managers gave more specific answers:

In other jobs I have had more specific targets to achieve. Now I have more choice as there are less clear criteria on which to measure success.
Systems controller

It is a more cross-divisional job with wider responsibilities. Previously I was a regional manager. This job gives a more initiating role; it is less reactive.
Marketing manager at head office

It's a new job, so it's what I make it.
Market and product development manager

It's a green field situation, so I can set my own systems and my own climate.
Commissioning engineer

I can use a much wider field of engineering because there are so few engineers in the factory, and therefore I feel I'm a specialist. I provide a service which I think is needed, and I think this gives one a great deal of freedom.
Engineer who had previously worked in a large engineering department in another company

I tend to feel liberated in this job compared to the last one. Most of my working day I can decide what to do . . . there's time in which I can sit back, read, try and think about the business. Very different from one level down, where I seemed to be swamped from morning to night with things that had to be done.
Product manager

A marketing manager, also in charge of sales, who felt that he had much more choice in his present job gave a very detailed explanation of this:

I think that the freedom for choice in this job is dramatically increased on anything that I've ever done before. I think there are a number of reasons for that. One is the level at which this job is operating. I am head of a significant function in this business, having in principle at least a major contribution to make this business grow. The role and the job that I had before was as technical manager reporting to a technical director in a very much larger unit. I was very much more constrained. My freedom of decision was very very limited. That's one level. At another level is the question of personal interaction with one's boss. . . . He gives me the opportunity within the overall framework to play things the way that I want to play them, whereas before I had a boss who did the opposite . . .'

I think the area for choice, the area for flexibility, the area for one to determine the way that one wants to go, is greater, because all of us, including the managing director, are travelling up a learning curve . . . I think largely because we are small and we're growing very very rapidly.

Some managers gave more mixed replies in comparing opportunities for choice in their present job with their previous ones. They described the ways in which they felt that they now had less choice, as well as the ways in which they had more.

Sometimes I think I have less choice than in the previous job. I was then the only one with specific expertise. Now I am conscious of the need to work to requirements of peers and to run parallel to Transport. I am more conscious of the need to be right when committing the company to new equipment.

Warehouse manager

I have more choice to get on with the job and make changes; less in that I can't go round the country seeing other industries, looking at how others do things.

Production manager

I have less choice in that formerly as overseas general marketing manager I had total responsibility for everything that moved. This perception of choice was probably illusory, as I had guidelines. I have more choice in that I am in charge of a wider range of operations, but within a narrower field.

Marketing manager in charge of a major product

A process and development engineer who was in charge of a particular project contrasted the freedom he had in this job compared with his previous one as works engineer. In his current job he could decide how to make the project profitable. He could decide whether he spent an hour on the nuts and bolts of the process they were developing or a few days with customers to develop the sales. 'That's a wonderful freedom and I'm thoroughly enjoying that.' When he was works engineer he had to deal with adverse reactions from the shop floor. 'Everything was predictable: just one hard slog of clearing day-to-day problems.'

This manager illustrates the ambivalence that some of the more analytical managers felt about the opportunities for choice. After describing some of the choices above he commented at the end of the interview that, when walking over for it, he thought: 'I don't have any choice at all.' He explained:

You can choose for a whole month, if you want, without talking to people; then you get into the management system, it's got to be very controlled, professional, right. That means the choice isn't yours. It's got to be the choice of a very complex interrelated system. So choice is negligible if I think of it that way.

69

A few managers thought there was no difference in how much choice they had in different jobs because their approach would always give them choice:

I've always felt in management jobs that I had the freedom I've needed. Never been turned back. Perhaps my way of getting things done—every sneaky way you can.

Production manager

Choice was seen by some managers as a characteristic of a particular job; by others as something that you earned by getting your boss to trust your competence, and by a few managers, particularly by those in one manufacturing company, as something that you made for yourself by finding your way round policies and procedures. The freedom that you earned from getting your boss's trust was most frequently mentioned in one of three manufacturing companies studied in the fifth research project. In another, a large complex organization, constraints were seen to come from the systems, from peers, from the frequent meetings, and from industrial relations, and not so much from the boss.

Choices over time in a job

Some managers said that they were more conscious of the opportunities for choice when they were new in a job:

I am more conscious of the choices because I am new in the job. In my previous job I realize that I was making similar choices but not thinking so much about them as a lot of established precedent to draw on. Just did it. Now I am conscious of choice and pretty wary of finding myself slipping into something without thinking. It won't last; I am trying to say to myself: 'get things right at the beginning, otherwise you are going to establish precedents'.

Laboratory manager

Others felt that in the early period in the job they were so busy getting to know it, trying to keep on top of the demands, that they had no time to think about opportunities for choice. It was only when they felt more in control of the job that they could do so. The more analytical and initiating managers were inclined to consider at the start what choices the job offered.

Many managers commented upon how choices change over time in a job:

I'm a new boy so I haven't managed to explore all the choices. They evolve over time.

Marketing manager

I think the choices have increased progressively. I think you recognize how things might be better done, how you might organize things better to give yourself more scope for manoeuvre. It is not just a case of having a higher position in the organization, therefore more authority, but getting attuned to the sort of environment where you need to carve out manoeuvring room for yourself.

Engineering services manager

Both these managers are describing an increase in choice after one has been in the job some time, but they do not say whether there comes a time when one sees less choice. One might expect that this would be so because of the concern that is expressed about people getting stale after some years in a job. This seems to be true for some managers, particularly those who started their jobs with plans for what they wanted to do. After a time, as one general manager put it, 'one has done it all, and only fine tuning remains'. This is not a universal reaction. Some managers, who have spent many years in the same job, say that they have the choice of managing their unit in their own way and apparently remain satisfied with that. The difference between these two views may be explained by whether one gets satisfaction from being responsible for changing the situation or for competently maintaining it.

Steering or carried along?

A manager is traditionally described as someone who does the planning, as well as carrying out the other functions of management, such as organizing and motivating, that have been repeated over the years in management textbooks. To plan one must consider what one's objectives are and how they can be attained. Such planning means reviewing the choices that are available. Yet most of the managers whom we studied, or with whom we have worked on courses, say that they are not normally conscious of choice. This might suggest that they are carried along, reacting to things that happen, rather than deliberately trying to steer; or, to put it more positively, they are relying on their training and experience to do the work that presents itself, rather than consciously weighing up what it is that they ought to be doing and what they want to do. Our research and work with managers shows that such a bald statement as 'managers are carried along' is an over-simplification. It is a useful corrective to the unrealistic emphasis on managers as planners, but we need to recognize the extent of individual differences both in overall approach to the job and in the way various aspects of the job are handled.

Managers may steer their work by having a personal policy for the way in which they should approach a job, that is, beliefs or guidelines about how to manage. They may also do so by having specific plans for what they are trying to achieve, which can be for the job as a whole as well as for particular aspects of it. Some managers in discussing choice described their broad approach to the job. There was the production manager, quoted at the start of the chapter, who tried to operate as if there were no constraints. Other examples of a general approach are:

My personal approach is to get it done correctly; so perhaps it will take a little bit longer, but in the long run you're going to save time.

Senior production engineer

Got to school myself to try and become at least adequate in day-to-day choices and settle into a situation where those are made not exactly automatically but fairly quickly and efficiently. Then get back to the big ones. Have a feeling other people aren't like that, don't get involved in the big decisions, happy having a working day of lots of small ones.

Laboratory manager

The main thing is delegation, freeing you to be able to look at other things that you probably wouldn't have time to do if you were doing their job for them.

Section engineer

Some managers volunteered their beliefs and guidelines for handling relationships. Most common were guidelines for handling one's boss or managing one's subordinates:

You must learn what your boss's buying habits are.

One has got to get the measure of what one's immediate superior is really looking for in you and in the job.

I think that by and large a democratic approach leads to a happier environment and better results.

You have got to encourage them so far, let them swim for themselves, but have also got to ensure that there's regular monitoring to make sure they don't hurt themselves.

Manager of young engineers

or generally how to treat people:

You mustn't be frank with some people because you know the reaction you will get, so tiptoe.

The other way in which managers may try to steer their jobs is by having specific plans for them. Plans differ from the broad approach described above in that they are related to a particular situation, rather than being the guidelines that a manager brings to any job. In the fifth research project we asked managers whether they had a plan for their job. Most said 'no'. Those who said 'yes' made statements like:

At this moment I'm trying to apply some administrative ability to getting some systems into the production engineering department, so that we can monitor readily, on a sort of day-to-day or week-to-week basis, the load against capacity. So I'm tending to move from the engineering, which is the bit that I really enjoy, to a more administrative role.

I do normally tend to have a plan for a job. It always develops very early in my mind: whether the structure of the department is right to cope with the known work load.

I build up a plan in a new job of what I'm going to do over the next few years. It's a series of hurdles, you do it to the best of your ability as quickly as you can and then look for the next hurdle.

Some of those who said they did not have a plan described plans for part of their work, such as developing one of their subordinates or trying to improve a particular system. The most common plan reported was to determine when one would do different tasks. The usual aim was to establish immediate priorities so as to try and ensure that the most urgent tasks got done. The conclusion seems to be that many managers will try to plan at least some aspect of their work, even if it is only what tasks should be tackled today.

We also asked the middle managers in the fifth research project whether they had a plan for their career. Most said that they did not. For some this was because they thought that they were unlikely to get any further or did not want to do so, but for others it seemed to be because they felt no career initiative on their part was appropriate. Some thought that career decisions should be left to their seniors. Some said that they did not think about careers but lived in the present. Whatever the reason, most did not think about what they could do to advance their careers. Of course, there were exceptions to this lack of career planning. The managers who were most aware of opportunities for choice in jobs tended also to think about career choices: in both, they had thought out what their policy ought to be. Examples of this for careers and promotion are:

I go for rescue jobs, where one can only go upwards.

The job tends to run me when I'm young in it, when I feel that I'm really running the job, I then start to plan, how to make it look that I've been really successful so that I can be selected for the next one.

I have always been conscious of the job that was the next obvious job for myself. At this time I wouldn't consider that I was ready for a job with even wider choices. One doesn't just step from one job to the next; one moves through a job.

I think it is my duty to let the company know what I want.

We are now in a position to try to answer the question posed at the start of this section: 'Steering or carried along?' The analogy is not a perfect one because the picture that we have presented is more complex. Managers may steer in some aspects of their jobs and not in others. But broadly one can say, from the experience of the fifth research study and of the courses, that the majority of these managers did not have an overall plan for the job. This does not mean that they were not trying to meet whatever objectives they had been set, but rather that they were not consciously planning how to do so. Nor were they trying to plan, or steer, their careers.

The information given here comes mainly from middle and upper-middle managers and only from British managers. It may be that senior managers have more need for, and are also more inclined to develop, plans. It is harder for them to do their jobs in a predominantly responsive way. The study of 41 district administrators in the National Health Service in the fourth research project gives us some comparative material from those in a senior post. Among that group we found more who did have a well articulated plan for what they were trying to achieve over all and for how to do this in different parts of their job. But the range was still very wide between those who were primarily reactive and those who had long-term and very explicit plans.

This chapter has concentrated upon how individual managers see, or do not consider, opportunities for choice in their jobs. It has not discussed how far demands, constraints, and choices are peculiar to the individual and therefore differ for different individuals in the same job. We discussed these individual differences briefly in Chapter 1, emphasizing the variations that there may be in other people's expectations of what they will do. Individuals may determine the demands, constraints, and choices in two main ways. One is by actually changing the job; by reducing or increasing the demands or constraints and thus affecting the choices available. Some jobs are too formalized for this to be possible, particularly if they are one of a class of similar well-defined jobs. Others, particularly new jobs, may be sufficiently flexible and undefined for the individual to be able to change, or even to determine, the nature of the job.

The other way in which individuals may determine the demands, constraints, and choices is by their own perception of them, so that the job is not changed but their perception of it gives them their own personal, distinctive, view of what they must do, cannot do, or can choose to do. Their view of the job will be influenced, too, by their own abilities, preferences, and weaknesses. One can think, therefore, of the demands, constraints, and choices inherent in the job, as well as of those that may be distinctive to the individual. The implications of these individual differences are considered in Chapters 11 and 12.

Summary

This chapter adopted a different perspective from the previous ones. Instead of looking at the nature of choices in managerial jobs, it described what managers said about the opportunities for choice in their jobs. Most of those studied said that they were normally unconscious of choosing what actions they took, or what decisions they made. They were carried along by the momentum of what happened. Most also said they had no plan for their jobs. However, their descriptions showed that most of them would have a plan for some part of their activities, if only in terms of priorities for the day's tasks.

A minority of the managers said that they were very aware of choosing. Some described their general approach to any managerial job including their beliefs about how to handle relationships. Some described specific plans for what they wanted to do in their job.

Even the managers who said that they were not usually conscious of making a choice described what aspects of a job and of its situation would give them choice. For most of them this was when other people did not tell them what to do, especially if they had their own defined area of responsibility within which they were free to manage as they thought best.

Most of the managers also said that they had no plan for their career. Those who were most aware of opportunities for choice in their jobs tended also to think about career choices.

PART THREE
Implications

9.

Different kinds of jobs

It is a real management job, which calls for innovation, motivation, drive, aggression.

Boss of project manager in charge of plant construction

The real criteria of success is what has changed as a result of his past year's activities.

Controller's boss

To me it's a flashing scenario which keeps changing every minute, at some stage I have to freeze the situation and say: 'Of all the hundreds of options open to me I like that one', and then be able to say why I have chosen it. It is difficult to be totally rational.

Financial controller

The company structure is a frustrating and stressful environment, bureaucratic and ponderous, but if a manager is prepared to stick his neck out and short-circuit the bureaucracy, show knowledge above his real level of authority, he can move things along and have a significant effect on the way the job operates.

Marketing director in an electronics company about his product managers

We talk about *the* managerial job, and business schools prepare students for management, but within this broad category there is a wide variety of jobs: jobs that require very different knowledge, skills and abilities; jobs that feel very different; jobs that differ widely in the nature and extent of their demands, constraints, and choices. The quotations above illustrate a few of these differences, and the last one also suggests some organizational influences on a job. How can these differences be *usefully* described and classified? This question has concerned the writer in several studies, both in this book and previously, which have sought to understand and to classify similarities and differences in managerial jobs. The word 'usefully' requires one to ask: 'Useful for whom?' and 'Useful for what?' My original hope was to develop a single typology to differentiate managerial jobs. There would be many advantages in being able to do that satisfactorily, but I now think that managerial jobs are too varied and consist of too many different aspects for that to be useful.[1] Rather, one needs to identify different characteristics for different purposes as well as to improve one's understanding of the similarities in managerial jobs. Other people have contributed to these tasks and more, it is hoped, will do so.[2]

The value of comparing managerial jobs may be doubted by those who think primarily in terms of *the* managerial job, so we shall start by reviewing the possible reasons for making comparisons. The main reasons are for:

- Job evaluation; determining the appropriate level of salary
- Job design and organizational design; that is, the number and kind of jobs that one should have and how they should be grouped together
- Selection; to determine what types of knowledge and abilities are required for different jobs
- Appraisals; in determining how performance can be assessed in different jobs
- Training; to know what kind of training may be necessary for an individual moving from a different type of job
- Career development; to know what kinds of experience different jobs can offer

Making comparisons between jobs is a necessary and frequent part of the work of personnel and training managers. It is a necessary, though less frequent, part of all managers' work. Making comparisons between jobs rarely receives the attention that it merits. It is only in job evaluation that considerable attention has necessarily been given to it, but the purposes of comparison, and hence the appropriate bases for it, are different from those needed for appraisal and training, and cover only some of those needed for selection. The range of characteristics that can and should be considered for selection, appraisal, and training is wider than for job evaluation.

Ways of comparing jobs

Post-experience management training recognizes a few differences between the training needs of managers in different jobs. There are the broad divisions by function for specialist training and by level in the hierarchy. Two career transitions are also commonly seen as times when training is desirable: the first is on promotion to a job with supervisory responsibilities; the second is on promotion from departmental head to a senior management post that requires a view wider than that of the particular function. Management training rarely

1. The few overall typologies that have been produced, although they are interesting attempts, illustrate the limitations of doing do, particularly when the problems discussed in Chapter 10 on the need to distinguish managerial work, behaviour, and perceptions are taken into account. The most highly developed examples of typologies are Hemphill (1960) and Tornow and Pinto (1976).

2. The most seminal of these contributions are: Carlson (1951), Sayles (1964), Mintzberg (1973), and Kotter (1982).

takes account of other variations between jobs, yet the identification of training needs requires a good understanding of the characteristics of individual jobs, and of the abilities and skills that they require. Those involved in training managers from different organizations also need some understanding of the variations in jobs caused by organizational differences.

A number of different divisions have been made of the abilities, knowledge, and skills required in managerial jobs. There is the simple and widely quoted distinction made by Katz (1955) between technical, human, and conceptual skills. A more elaborate analysis was put forward by Burgoyne and Stuart (1976), who proposed ten characteristics which included those cited by Katz and others such as emotional resilience.

	Analytical abilities					Social skills					Emotional resilience		
Extent to which required	Strategic decisions	Boundary management	Assessment of own strengths & weaknesses	Assessment of others	Super- vision	Boss	Peers	Exter- nal contacts	Group working	Exposure	Ambiguity in decision- taking	Inter- personal con- straint
	1 For unit · 2 Own work												
Very high													
High													
Mod.													
Low													
Little or none													

Fig. 9.1   *Dimensions for comparing some of the analytical abilities, social skills, and emotional resilience required in different jobs*
1.Common requirements in all managerial jobs

The studies on which this book and its predecessor were based contribute to understanding three of Burgoyne's categories, two of which are the same as Katz's: analytical, problem-solving, and decision/judgement-making skills; social skills and abilities; and emotional resilience. We shall limit our discussion to these three. Technical skills, though important, are not included because our research does not contribute to their understanding. Nor is it so useful for it to do so, as more attention is generally given to technical skills.

Figures 9.1–9.3 illustrate how the three broad groups, 'analytical abilities', 'social skills', and 'emotional resilience', can be used to compare jobs. Each of the three has a number of subdivisions. The vertical scale in the figures is an approximate guide to the extent to which each of these dimensions applies in the job. For some of these dimensions we have more information on which to base our estimates than for others.

The first two subdivisions of analytical abilities are for different kinds of 'strategic decisions'. The first is for those about the nature of the unit's output. Chapter 4, on choices of unit domain, argued that one of the important differences between jobs is whether the jobholder has the choice of determining or modifying what is done by the unit for which he or she is responsible.

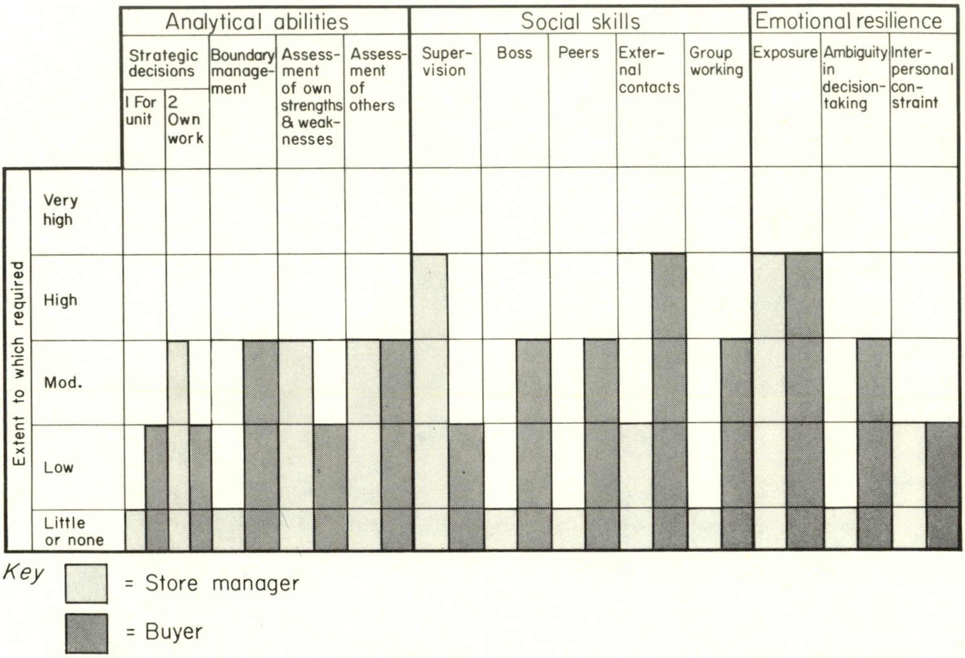

	Analytical abilities					Social skills					Emotional resilience		
Extent to which required	Strategic decisions		Boundary management	Assessment of own strengths & weaknesses	Assessment of others	Super-vision	Boss	Peers	External contacts	Group working	Exposure	Ambiguity in decision-taking	Inter-personal constraint
	1 For unit	2 Own work											
Very high													
High													
Mod.													
Low													
Little or none													

Key
☐ = Store manager
▨ = Buyer

Fig. 9.2 Dimensions for comparing some of the analytical abilities, social skills, and emotional resilience required in different jobs
2. Comparison of a store manager's and buyer's jobs in a retail chain store

The examples given in that chapter show that, although one would expect this choice to be more common at the senior management level, it can also be found in jobs lower down, particularly in many staff jobs. The second dimension for strategic decisions is for one's own work. Chapter 2, on common choices, showed that in all managerial jobs there is some choice in what the manager does and, therefore, some opportunity for strategic thinking about that. Chapter 5, on choices of personal domain, showed that in some jobs the choices are so wide that much of the time can be spent on different work by managers in similar jobs. In such jobs managers need to think strategically about what they should be doing.

The third heading under analytical abilities is 'boundary management'. Chapter 3 argued that in many of their jobs managers have a choice of trying to understand and influence the factors that can affect the operation of their units. Boundary management is listed as an analytical ability because of the need to identify both what external factors are important to the effective running of the unit and also how they might be modified. The first may require no analytical ability as the need may be glaringly obvious, but analysis will usually be needed to decide what should be done about it. Successful boundary management will often require interpersonal skills as well.

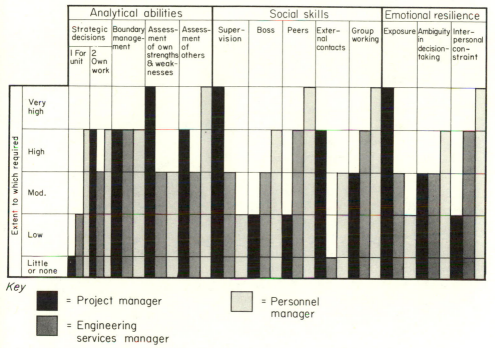

Fig. 9.3 *Dimensions for comparing some of the analytical abilities, social skills, and emotional resilience required in different jobs*
3. Comparison of project manager, engineering services manager, and personnel manager in a large chemical company

The remaining two headings under analytical abilities require emotional detachment as well as intellectual ability. The first is the 'capacity to assess one's own strengths and weaknesses', because that is important in deciding what choices one should make in the work that one does. The second is the 'capacity to assess the actual and potential contribution that is, and can be, made by others'. The importance of these two is shown by our evidence of the amount of choice that exists in managerial jobs and hence the need for

83

jobholders to decide what they can most effectively do. This is most necessary in jobs where there is a wide choice in the work that can be done, and in those where work can be shared in different ways upwards, downwards, and horizontally between the members of a management team.

The second broad group in the figures is 'social skills'. The first four headings are taken from the analysis in *Contrasts in Management* (Stewart, 1976), which showed that jobs differ both in the contacts that they require and in their relative difficulty. Contacts are divided into 'subordinates', 'boss', people in other departments called 'peers', and 'external contacts'. Some jobs do not require all these types of contact. The position of a job on each of these four divisions in the figures is determined by the relative difficulty of the required relationships. *Contrasts in Management* described how one could assess the inherent difficulty of each of these relationships in different jobs, irrespective of the particular personalities.

The social skills group contains two other subdivisions, which were not considered in *Contrasts in Management*. The first is 'group working', where the job involves being part of one or more teams of people. Jobs vary considerably in the extent to which this is a necessary component of the job and in the nature and amount of social skills that are required. Our studies did not assess this, so the estimates given in Figs. 9.1, 9.2, and 9.3 are based only on our observations in the third and fourth studies. The second of these additional headings in social skills is 'serving political masters', which is a distinctive characteristic of some of the more senior jobs in public service. It is not included in the figures as it does not apply to the jobs shown there.

The headings give a broad indication of the kinds of social skills that will be necessary, but one will often want to know what specific skills are required. Supervisory skills, for example, will be somewhat different for the head of a research team from a production supervisor in a mass production plant.

The third group is 'emotional resilience', which means that the job requires an individual to be able to tolerate certain potentially stressful aspects. The first division is 'exposure', which was described in *Contrasts in Management* as a job where the individual must run the risk of being known to have performed badly or to have made mistakes. Some jobs are more exposed than others and some are not exposed at all, as we showed in *Contrasts in Management*. This characteristic was found in some junior and middle management jobs and not in all senior management posts. Indeed, in some organizations it would be less common at the senior levels, where decisions are often group ones.

The remaining categories are different aspects of ambiguity. The first is called 'ambiguity in decision-taking' and is concerned with the need to select between uncertain alternatives. It is the ambiguity illustrated in the quotation from the financial controller at the start of the chapter. There is probably some aspect of it in all managerial jobs, though in some it will be very small and in a few it can be very large. The reasons for the ambiguity will vary and may occur at different stages in decision-taking. The second of the ambiguous categories is called 'interpersonal constraints', where the jobholder's actions are constrained by need to work with, and consult, many different people. The effect of this constraint upon a manager's sense of the opportunities for choice was illustrated in the previous chapter.

Different forms of comparison are useful for different purposes. The ones that are illustrated in the figures can be used for selection to consider how well an individual is likely to be able to meet these requirements, and for appraisal in reviewing how far he or she is doing so. Their main value may be to help in considering the kind of training that would be appropriate for the holders of jobs with different profiles on the dimensions illustrated. The dimensions do not attempt to cover all possible aspects of a job, but using them to compare jobs would highlight some differences in training needs. However, the kind of training that would be appropriate will vary for different dimensions. Probably emotional resilience can be developed only by experience and coaching, not by courses.

Figure 9.1 suggests that there are few common training requirements for these abilities and skills across all managerial jobs. (The argument for such low rating of supervisory requirements in some jobs is substantiated in *Contrasts in Management*.) Figures 9.2 and 9.3 illustrate the argument that, to identify the abilities, social skills, and emotional resilience required in particular jobs, it is not sufficient to know whether they are junior, middle, or senior management. This is especially true, our research suggests, for middle management jobs. It is somewhat easier to generalize about the analytical abilities required in top management jobs because of the greater range of choice that they offer in unit domain and personal domain than most managerial jobs lower down in the same organization. Top management jobs do in general require at least moderate abilities for each of the analytical dimensions in the figures. Many of them require high abilities for each. This is a justification for the corporate policy teaching to senior management, which aims to help them to take strategic decisions. However, such teaching is mainly addressed to the analytical thinking needed in the first column, that is, strategic thinking for the unit, and to some extent to that required in boundary management. The strategic thinking needed about what work the individual should be doing rarely receives the attention that it requires in jobs offering a wide choice.

Examples of job comparisons

Figure 9.2 compares a store manager and knitwear buyer at the same level in the same retail chain store company. A glance at the profiles on the figure will show the similarities and differences, which are explained below. The store manager's job is primarily a supervisory one. The main training need is to ensure that store managers are good at managing their staff. There is a moderate need for them to think strategically about giving greater emphasis to staff management, merchandising or administration. There is a related choice in the amount and nature of delegation, so they should have some understanding of their own strengths and weaknesses. The extent of their staff management responsibilities, including the number of their staff and the importance of developing other managers, means that they should also be able to assess others.

The buyer's job resembles that of the store manager in three main ways. Perhaps most importantly for how the job feels is that both jobs are well defined: the area of discretion is clear. Both are also exposed, because their performance can be assessed and the mistakes of the buyer will be known. Both also require some capacity to assess others, though for the buyer this applies mainly to suppliers. Otherwise the buyer's job differs in many respects. There is a relatively small element of staff management and a wider range of contacts. The job is a more political one, as it is based at head office and involves working with other departments there. There is a little more scope for strategic decisions about the unit's work within the constraints of the company's product policies. Changes in consumer taste and variations in weather lead to some ambiguity in decision-taking, though in knitwear these are not of great importance. The jobs differ markedly in the depth of technical knowledge required, but this, unlike the kind of differences shown in Fig. 9.2, is likely to be adequately recognized.

The profile of the retail chain store manager on Fig. 9.2 is typical of managers of similar branches of large organizations, such as banks, post offices, and building societies. The main variations will be in the importance of external contacts and in whether there is any scope for strategic decisions about the nature of the work that is done by the unit. One striking difference between such jobs and those that are found in larger units and at head offices is that they require less varied skills. Jobs in charge of such separate units do not have the political component that is inherent in much managerial work where the jobholder has to try and get the cooperation of people in other departments. Because of this, they are not subject to as many interpersonal constraints. They do not have the same uncertainties about what they can do. They tend, as we saw in Chapter 8, to have a greater sense of freedom.

Figure 9.3 compares three management jobs at the same hierarchical level in a very different kind of company, a large chemical works. These are called 'senior management', though below the top levels. Two of the jobs are in the engineering department: a project manager in charge of a large construction site, and an engineering services manager. The other is a personnel manager. The jobs differ in some important respects from each other but they differ even more from both jobs in the retail chain store, as a comparison of Figs. 9.2 and 9.3 will show. They have higher requirements on many of the dimensions than either of the two retailing jobs because they work in a large matrix organization where responsibilities are less clear-cut and there are more fluid and more political relations with people in other departments.

The project manager's job differs markedly from either of the other two jobs represented on Fig. 9.3. It is an unusual job in the chemical company because it is more like being in charge of a separate business. The manager is responsible for building, with the assistance of outside contractors, a large chemical plant to given specifications by a certain date. The task is more clear-cut than that of the holders of the other two jobs. This is why the job is rated low for strategic decisions about the work that his unit should do. The end product is clearly established. The task is to ensure that it is achieved within the specifications set, including those of cost. It is an unusual job in any organization in that the work goes through different stages that require rather different abilities. Hence it is particularly important that the project manager has a good assessment of his or her own strengths and weaknesses in relation to these different phases, and a capacity to assess those of others. High supervisory skills are needed to carry the project through to the end while meeting the criteria set. The project manager must analyse the different external factors that may interfere with the progress of the project: boundary management must be good, which will require both analytical ability and interpersonal skills. The jobholder must be able to live with the very high level of exposure that goes with the job. The job can require other qualities, too, which are suggested in the first quotation at the start of the chapter.

The other engineering management job illustrated in Fig. 9.3 differs in many ways from that of the project manager. The engineering services manager is responsible for an ongoing service and works in parallel with the production manager. The post does not give the relative independence of the project manager. It is much more enmeshed in the matrix organization, so that it requires higher skills in peer relations. It is subject to considerably more constraint from working with other people, and the holder must be able to tolerate that without losing interest in taking initiatives. This post permits some changes in the work that is done by subordinates so there is a little more need for strategic thinking about the department's activities, but it is only at the margin rather than of prime importance in the job.

The post of personnel manager differs from both the engineering posts in having much less precisely defined objectives. There is, therefore, much more need for strategic thinking about the nature of the work that should be done. The lack of a measurable output makes the job much less exposed than the others. Whether it is exposed at all will depend upon the state of industrial relations and on how the personnel manager is involved. There are some personnel management jobs where industrial relations can mean high exposure on occasions. The personnel manager can have considerable choice over the work in which he or she personally gets involved, and so needs to think strategically about that.

The personnel manager's job resembles that of the engineering services manager in some of the dimensions in Fig. 9.3, but there are also differences. There is a greater need to be able to assess others which could be described as part of the professional expertise. The job requires more skill in working with peers because the personnel manager is offering a less valued and needed service and hence has to be more skilful at enlisting the cooperation of others and at persuading them to make changes. This means that a very high level of skill in group working is needed in a company where meetings are the custom. The personnel manager's relative lack of power makes the job even more subject than that of the engineering services manager to the constraints that come from having to work with others who can limit or negate what one is trying to do.

Summary

The argument in this and preceding chapters is that, for improved selection, appraisal, and training, we need to have a better understanding of the nature of managerial jobs. This chapter was intended to help those who need to make comparisons between jobs, and who are willing to recognize that jobs vary in other ways than by level in the hierarchy and by technical knowledge and skill. Three broad categories were used to show how jobs could be compared: analytical abilities, social skills, and emotional resilience. Each of these was subdivided on the basis of our research studies. The aim was to go beyond broad generalizations about the qualities that managers need to compare how jobs differ in the qualities that they require. Illustrations were given of comparisons between jobs at the same level and in the same company.

10.
Implications for teachers and researchers

This chapter will suggest the implications of the four research projects on which this book is based for management studies teachers, for some aspects of teaching in organizational behaviour, and for researchers in the fields of managerial behaviour, managerial work, managerial attitudes, leadership, and in some other aspects of organizational behaviour research. The research suggestions will include fruitful areas for future work and some cautions about methodology.

The studies developed and applied a model—that of demands, constraints, and choices—that can be used to explore:

– The nature of managerial jobs, and other responsible jobs as well
– How an individual perceives his or her job
– The behaviour of the jobholder

The studies also produced a variety of findings about the nature of managerial jobs, about managerial behaviour, and managerial perceptions that have implications for teaching and research. The implications for the organization and for the individual manager are discussed in separate chapters. The main findings are summarized below.

1. All managerial jobs offer opportunities for choosing what is done, as well as how it is done.
2. There are some common opportunities for choice that characterize all managerial jobs, and some others that characterize most of them. Thus some generalizations can be made.
3. Managerial jobs also differ in the nature of the opportunities for choice that they provide. These differences can be described, and some of them, at least, can be measured.
4. These differences cut across those of function and level, showing that these are not, for certain purposes, a sufficient way of differentiating between managerial jobs. The implications for selection, appraisal, and training are discussed in Chapter 12.
5. Some managerial jobs offer so much choice that holders in similar jobs can spend much of their time doing different kinds of work.

6. In some jobs the opportunities to share work with other people, especially other members of a management team, mean that for some purposes it is inadequate to consider either the job or the performance of the jobholder on their own.
7. Individual managers can have very different perceptions of the nature of their jobs.
8. (a) Most of the managers studied were, according to them, intuitive responders rather than strategic planners.
    (b) There were large individual variations in whether, and if so the areas in which, managers reported an analytical approach to their jobs.

The evidence for these findings is in part contained in this book, including Appendix 1 on the research methods, and in part, more formally, in Stewart, Smith, Blake and Wingate (1980), Stewart (1981), and Marshall and Stewart (1981a,b). The findings are based on studies of a few hundred British managers and administrators, so one must ask whether the generalizations above are justified, and whether they are likely to apply outside the UK. There seems no reason to think that the first seven findings listed are not generally applicable to managers anywhere. The last finding is worded more restrictively because the evidence cannot tell us either how widely it would apply to a quite different group of managers in the UK, or whether there would be cross-cultural differences. However, studies in Sweden (Carlson, 1951) and in the USA (Mintzberg, 1973) suggest that managers elsewhere may also commonly be intuitive responders rather than strategic planners.

Implications for teaching

Undergraduate and postgraduate education

The teaching of medicine provides useful parallels for examining the teaching of management. Both are arts as well as sciences; both require experience to supplement formal teaching. Medicine is more of a science than management, as one cannot practice it without a long period of formal teaching; yet the teaching of management at the undergraduate and postgraduate level is usually much more academic than the teaching of medicine.

Different approaches are used in some institutions to try and overcome the unduly theoretical nature of management studies, including the introduction of sandwich courses and the restriction of entry to postgraduate schools to those who have had several years' experience in industry or commerce. These are helpful ways of ensuring some understanding of organizational, though not necessarily of managerial, life. The limitation is that such management experience is usually much narrower and more haphazard than in medical training. It can do little to help the student to understand the variety of managerial work and the diversity of managerial behaviour. Various teaching methods, particularly case studies, projects in companies, and business games, can help to make managerial problems more real. However, they can also be misleading, by suggesting that much managerial work is taken up with decisions and with the analysis of problems. Management education gives little feel for what it is like to be a manager. Medical education is superior in giving the student a feel for what it is like to be a doctor both from observation and practice.

Students should be taught about the nature and diversity of managerial work and behaviour. They should be helped to recognize what sort of jobs are likely to suit them and what role models they prefer, and why. Such a course should include the study of the relatively small literature on the subject of management in practice and, possibly, the better biographies and auto-biographies, though these are mainly restricted to describing large-scale successful entrepreneurs. Students should be given some exposure to different kinds of managerial jobs and to different styles of management. This would be difficult to organize for very large classes, which may have to use specially written case studies, but wherever possible there should be fieldwork. Students might, for example, be asked to write comparative case studies of two different kinds of managerial jobs and of two managers in similar jobs using the model of demands constraints and choices as the basis to help them to understand differences in jobs and in behaviour. Even if the teachers are unable or unwilling to organize the necessary contacts, students should be able to arrange their own through family, friends, or their own initiative. Business schools that have programmes for middle or senior managers running at the same time offer other opportunities for students to gain an understanding of managerial work.

Post-experience teaching

The diversity of managerial work described in this book, and in its predecessor, *Contrasts in Management,* should make management trainers and those in post-experience management education more concerned about the relevance of what is taught to managers in very different kinds of jobs. The assumption that all managers need to know X or would be helped by being better at Y should be examined more often than it is. It is true that for the sake of convenience management trainers will often operate—indeed, need to operate—as if such assumptions are true; but they should also be thinking about differences in training needs. So far the commonly recognized differences are those of level in the hierarchy and, less frequently, function. Our researches suggest that other job differences are also important for identifying training needs. Chapter 9 illustrated some of the training needs in different types of jobs. One job difference is whether strategic thinking is required about what goods or services the manager's unit should be producing. Another is the extent to which the jobholders can determine what work they do themselves. The greater the flexibility in the job, the greater the need for the manager to think strategically about what he or she can do more effectively. Chapters 4 and 5 described the opportunities for strategic thinking in different jobs. Another difference between jobs that is relevant for training is the nature and difficulty of the manager's contacts (Stewart, 1976).

Far fewer of the managers who took part in the research project on perceptions of choice, or in the courses on managerial work, appeared to have thought about their relations with colleagues, bosses, or people outside the organization than about their relations with their subordinates. This suggests that management trainers may give too little attention to these other relationships. It may be easier to help managers here, as beliefs about how these relationships should be handled are less developed and solidified than are those for subordinate management. Exercises 3 and 9 in Appendix 3 can be used to stimulate managers to think about these relationships. Managers can also be helped by training in trading skills (Knibbs, 1975). An understanding of organizational politics is important in some jobs, particularly the more senior ones. Sessions on this topic have for some years been one of the most popular at the Oxford Centre for Management Studies.

Chapter 8, on 'How managers see choice', showed considerable differences between managers in whether they thought analytically about their jobs and about what they should be doing, or primarily were responding instinctively to events as they occurred. The latter was more common among the managers studied. Yet much management training tends to assume implicitly that managers are analytical and goal-oriented and that what is needed is information that will improve their analysis. This is, the research suggests, unrealistic. If it is, management trainers need to consider the implications. Should they be trying to make more managers analytical about their work and more concerned with setting and pursuing priorities? If they think the answer is 'yes', they may find the exercises given in Appendix 3 helpful. Management by objectives has had this purpose, but its often formal character means that the individual is not stimulated to examine his or her own approach to the job. Two managers listing the same objectives may still do the job very differently.

Management trainers should also consider the training implications of the habit formation that underlies the instinctive reactions described in Chapter 8. The first few years, perhaps just the first few months, in a managerial job may have great importance in determining the kind of habits of managing that are developed. If this is so—and whether it is needs to be researched—the early training should be a prime concern of the management trainer. Courses for newly appointed managers may be helpful in telling them some of the things to look out for and in providing skills training, but what the managers learn on the job is likely to be a far more important influence in determining habit formation than any course. The new manager's boss may play a critical role. Hence management trainers in an organization should learn which managers are interested in coaching and are good at it and try to ensure that as many new managers as possible get experience working for them. However, the organization needs to recognize the contribution made by such managers so that they are compensated for the disadvantages of having an unduly high proportion of learners. The importance of coaching suggests the desirability of providing courses to help managers to become better coaches.

Another training implication of managers' instinctive reactions is the need to help them when they are newly appointed to a job. This is the time when managers are most likely to be interested in thinking about what they should do. The model of demands, contraints, and choices provides a good means of helping them to do so. If they can work in a small group with two other managers to act as catalysts to their thinking about the job, they will get a wider perception of its possibilities than they will working on their own. In our experience most managers make very good catalysts for other managers, and find it interesting and useful to them even though they are discussing another person's job. Managers in different types of jobs are more searching in their questions than those in similar jobs who may take too much for granted.

Implications and suggestions for research
(This section is only likely to be of interest to academics)

The implications for research are diverse, and provide suggestions for those with very different interests both of subject and of methodology. Naturally, the main implications are for further research in managerial work and behaviour. There are also suggestions for those who are interested primarily in organizations rather than in individuals. The implications for leadership studies are considered briefly, and there is a suggestion for research on boundary roles.

Managerial work, behaviour and perceptions

Progress in our understanding of managerial work and behaviour has been handicapped by the neglect of two problems. The first is that of developing concepts to determine what aspects of work and behaviour should be studied. Hackman (1969), although writing about the problems of understanding tasks in behavioural research, can still be taken as a guide to thinking about the formidable (from the conceptual point of view) multi-dimensionality of managerial work in a single job, and even more so in the wide variety of jobs that are called 'managerial'. Until more people are interested in seeking to tackle this problem of conceptual development, or at the very least recognize its existence, the study of managerial work and behaviour will not progress as it

93

should. It is unfortunate that the notable contribution made by Mintzberg (1973) is too often treated in the USA in a rather arid manner; too much attention is given to trying to measure and assess his general and abstract roles, rather than using his insights to further develop our conceptual understanding of the nature, complexity, and diversity of managerial work and behaviour. One example of the many suggestions in his book is to study the programmes that managers use. The ideas in the seminal book on managerial behaviour by Sayles (1964) have not been followed up in the way that they merit.

Kotter (1982) and Lombardo and McCall (1981) have made significant contributions to our conceptual thinking about managerial work and behaviour, but the field needs more people who are interested in doing that. Kotter, for example, in a study of 15 general managers in the USA, has called into question the transferability of general managers from one type of general management to another. This is an important corrective to the generalizations made about managerial work and behaviour, which has implications for recruitment, training, and promotion policies. It may help to explain why companies who are successful in one kind of business often fail when they enter another: the knowledge and skills required are more distinctive than they recognized. Kotter's findings illustrate the need to look at jobs and behaviour in greater depth. Mintzberg's roles are so general that they cannot tell us about the transferability of managerial knowledge and skills. Following Kotter, this is an important area for further investigation.

The second problem, whose neglect has handicapped progress in our understanding of managerial work and behaviour, is the frequent confusion between managerial work, which is used as a synonym for 'the job', managerial behaviour, and perceptions of the job. Researchers, management writers, and also managers themselves need to be clear about which they are looking at and what assumptions they are making when they say that one is a description of the other. The danger of generalizing from perceptions to behaviour is well known, though not as often remembered as it should be. The less recognized danger is of generalizing from behaviour to work. The evidence provided by our studies of differences in the behaviour of mangers in similar jobs underlie the importance of this distinction.

Mintzberg (1973) suggested a number of propositions about the characteristics of managerial work. Many of these were actually statements about managerial behaviour and not necessarily about managerial work. There is a need to test in what situations they are true. How many of his propositions apply, for example, to managers in similar jobs? Such a comparison would give some information about the individual variations that are possible. This is an important test of generalizations, as shown in our fourth study, where we found very great variations both in content and method among administrators in similar jobs.

We need to explore further the variations to be found in different kinds of jobs and of organizations. Such comparative studies can help us to identify what generalizations are appropriate in what situations, and which ones, if any, can be made more globally about managerial work and/or managerial behaviour. The studies described in this book and in its predecessor, *Contrasts in Management* (Stewart, 1976), have identified some of the differences between jobs, but there are others to be found by looking at different aspects of jobs.

We have little information about the organizational differences in managerial jobs and behaviour and of the reasons for them. There are a few suggestions in this book, and some propositions are put forward later in this chapter that could provide a starting point. A good research strategy could be carefully delimited comparative studies, perhaps starting with companies in the same kind of business.

Future studies should probably use different methods to make up for the limitations of any one method. There is a need for experiment with new methods to try and enrich our all too restricted and fallible tools. Questionnaires used alone are too limited a method to be likely to develop our concepts. There is a discussion of the qualitative methods used in these studies in Appendix 1.

It is important, whatever comparisons are made, to try and hold constant as many variables as possible. So far, little attention has been paid to this. Cross-cultural studies of managerial attitudes, for example, have with a few notable exceptions treated managers as equivalents, and argued that any variations could be attributed to cultural differences. Hofstede's studies of IBM managers in different countries are rare in being confined to one company (Hofstede, 1980). There is a need for studies that do seek to compare like with like, such as Graves's (1973) study of the behaviour of French and English managers in similar posts in very similar light electronic engineering factories.

The fifth research project, on managers' perceptions of opportunities for choice, found that an understanding of how managers see their jobs and themselves in them is a prerequisite to understanding what they say about a particular area of the job, in that instance the opportunities for choice. This suggests an important lesson to researchers that asking about some aspects of a job may not be meaningful unless the relevant context is already understood. To what extent this is true, and what that context is for a given project, can be adequately determined only by extensive exploration during the pilot stages of the research. Researchers using questionnaires should seek to find out at the pilot stage what the questions mean to different respondents. A useful check is to ask the same questions of managers in similar jobs.

A different area for future research is to learn more about the process of becoming a manager, and of how managerial beliefs and habits are formed. Longitudinal studies could be helpful here. The varied evidence that exists for a fragmented, responsive pattern of work among many, though not all, managers suggests that many managers must rely mainly upon the habitual forms of response that they have developed. How these are developed and, further, how, if it seems desirable, they can be changed are two potentially important areas for research that would be relevant to management training and to the kinds of job experience that managers should be given. The formation of managerial beliefs is another area for study; so is the nature of the beliefs and guidelines that managers use in tackling a job—in the fifth study we were struck by the frequency with which managers described these in our open-ended interviews, even though there were no questions about them.

The flexibility that our studies have shown in managerial jobs makes it even more important to consider what kind of behaviour is effective in what situations. Given that managers can and do behave so differently in similar jobs, what implications does this have for management effectiveness? Does it matter? It may be that the behaviour of managers is only a small part of what makes for organizational effectiveness. But selection and training policies assume that it is more important than that. So we need careful studies of the work done by individuals, pairs, and groups selected for differences in effectiveness, by whatever output or other measures are chosen. The studies of pairs and groups should also include how work is shared between different individuals.

Management dyads and groups

The sixth finding listed at the start of this chapter and discussed in Chapter 6 opens up some interesting and important topics for research that are different from the focus on individual jobs and on individual managers in the previous section. The fourth study, on the district administrator in the National Health Service, suggests a number of potentially fruitful areas for research in management groups. By 'group' is meant those who meet regularly to discuss the work of a particular organizational unit. The phrase 'management team' could be used instead, except for the different interpretations that are given to 'team'. Possible topics for research include the following:

– In what management groups does work-sharing develop?
– What kind of work is shared?
– What effects does the age of the group have on this?
– How soon after appointment do individuals start to share with others?
– Between which pairs does sharing commonly develop in particular groups?
– When, and for what purposes, does sharing go beyond two people?
– In what situations does sharing make for greater effectiveness?
– Is the answer different for the effectiveness of the group compared with that of the department for which the sharing managers are responsible?

These suggestions show that there are some interesting questions to be investigated in lateral dyads, and sometimes triads. They also show that there are many other aspects of the behaviour of managerial groups to be investigated beyond that of roles. There could be comparative studies of work-sharing in similar groups. Our fourth study, although it was only of one job in the management group, suggested the fruitful possibilities of such comparisons. A research area stemming from the demands, constraints, and choices model is to use it to examine group perceptions and behaviour by, for example, comparing how similar groups see the demands, constraints, and choices in their situation, and examining what work each group does and does not do.

Two examples of propositions that might be tested are:

1. More effective groups are those where the members work together on common problems rather than concentrating primarily on those of their own departments.
   (a) This is most true of groups experiencing changes in their environment.

Testing this proposition will require a definition of 'work together'.

2. Some positions in management groups give their holders more opportunities for lateral work-sharing than others.
   (a) Some positions give their holders a better knowledge base for understanding the work of other members.
   (b) Some positions give their holders greater access to information about the work of the group.
   (c) The holders of some jobs can play a more central role in encouraging work-sharing.

Measurement possibilities of the model

Here are some suggestions from these studies for researchers whose interests are in measurement. They indicate some of the more salient measurement possibilities of the model of demands, constraints, and choices. They range from some very simple measures that could be worth making for various purposes, such as comparing jobs in different functions or different organizations, to more complex and multi-dimensional measures.

Comparisons can be made between jobs or organizations of how much of a manager's time is taken up by demands that are intrinsic to the job and are not self-imposed. These would need to be assessed for particular jobs, but the following are common demands:

– Time spent in formal meetings, but distinguishing between those that have to be attended and those that are a choice
– Time spent in bureaucratic procedures that cannot be delegated

– Other regular tasks that cannot be delegated
– A minimum time that must be spent with each category of contacts

The common constraints described in Chapter 1 could also be measured. This can be more difficult to do than may at first appear because, as we found, of the variety of different factors that may be relevant to each constraint. Another and simpler approach to measuring constraints would be to compare how managers in different functions, levels, or companies rated the importance of different constraints. This would be a crude perceptual measure, not a comparison of the actual differences in constraints. The rating of different constraints could also be used to compare with perceptions of the amount and kinds of choice available.

A potentially intriguing, but difficult, subject for measurement is the amount of choice that different jobs offer. The difficulty would lie mainly in deciding what aspects of choice should be measured. A simple measure would be of the time that was not mortgaged by demands as measured in the ways suggested above. Marshall and Stewart (1981b) discuss estimates that managers gave of the amount of choice that their jobs offered. This is a crude perceptual measure, and one that might not accord with estimates made by an outsider. Interesting comparisons could be made between estimates of choice and the kinds of choices that the jobs were seen to offer. More complex measures could be made as suggested below of the size and variety of domains that the jobholder could occupy. Complex, but still feasible, measures could be made to determine the need for strategic thinking as illustrated in Exercise 1 in Appendix 3. This would require the following:

– Determining the extent to which the work for which the manager responsible has a specified output that can be measured. Scales could be developed to compare the number, specificity and frequency of measures.
– Determining the manager's domain, distinguishing between the unit's domain as discussed in Chapter 4, and the personal domain, as described in Chapter 5: this would be more complex to measure than the output specifications but simple scales could be developed for different aspects of the domain, starting for personal domain with the nature of work possibilities outside the unit, and outside the organization.

In any attempts to measure the research will need to be clear about what is being measured, whether it is individual perceptions, behaviour or the job.

Simple measures are likely to be more appropriate than more advanced statistical methods. The problem of the latter being applied to answers on complex subjects like managerial perceptions, behaviour and job characteristics is that they convey a misleading impression of accuracy: misleading because of the many meanings that those who answer questions may give to the statement to which they are responding; misleading, also, because many of the possible subjects for study are complex and one's measurements can cover only some of the aspects. Even extensive investigation may give one only a partial understanding of which are the more important ones.

There are decisions to be made about the type of measure to be used. Time and frequency are the measures that have most commonly been used in comparing managerial work and managerial behaviour, which is the more useful will depend upon the purpose. For some purposes other more ambiguous measures such as importance may be appropriate. The researcher will need to decide whether he or she is going to rely on estimates of these with their resultant inaccuracies, or to seek to get more accurate measures by observation, self-recording, secretarial records, and cross-checking with other people.

Leadership studies

The relevance of our researches for leadership studies has been described more fully elsewhere (Stewart, 1981), so we shall mention only the main suggestions for future research. Leadership studies have often been concerned with comparing and assessing different forms of leadership behaviour as described by subordinates in answer to standard questionnaires. The range of leadership behaviours has been narrowly conceived, and, except in the study of small groups, has concentrated upon manager and subordinates. There is a need to explore the leadership of people other than subordinates because ours, and other studies, show that many managers spend a considerable proportion of their contact time with peers, seniors, and people outside the organization. Studies should be made of who the manager is leading among the different contacts—upwards, sideways, and outwards as well as downwards. There may be occasions when the manager is leading the superior, although hierarchically minded people may find this difficult to accept. In considering leadership effectiveness, assessments need to be made of the relative difficulty and importance of these different contacts. Stewart (1976) showed how this could be done.

The evidence in this book of the flexibility of managerial work suggests that greater attention needs to be paid in leadership studies to the areas in which the manager is leading. The traditional leadership dichotomy between consideration and initiating structure does not distinguish within initiating structure. Yet effectiveness may crucially depend, particularly in the more flexible jobs, upon whether the work that the manager is initiating is what is most needed in the situation.

The disappointing history of leadership studies raises the query of whether the idea of leadership studies is an appropriate one. The fact that it is a value-laden concept may help to explain why the area of studies has been so narrowly focused and why, despite the large number of studies, more has not

99

been achieved. It may be more fruitful for the development of our understanding to change the focus from leadership to managerial work and behaviour, which seems more readily to encompass the wider subjects suggested above. Such a shift may be particularly useful for studying the more organic organizations, reserving the term 'leadership' for those settings, such as the military, where it may be more appropriate.

Organizational differences in the opportunities for choice

The organizational comparisons that were part of the original research design for the third research study were only partly completed because of the difficulty of getting cooperation in time from two matching companies. Hence no adequately tested generalizations can be put forward. However, the research did yield some suggestions about organizational differences as they affect both the nature of choices available in organizations and how managers perceive them. Because of the tentative nature of these findings, they are best put in the form of propositions. The ones listed below are suggestions for further research.

The structure and climate of the organization will affect the kind of choices that are available. This statement is too general to be useful except to indicate that organizational characteristics are one of the factors determining the nature of the opportunities for choice. More specifically, our research suggests the following.

1. A clearly defined area of choice will be seen as offering more opportunities for choice than a larger, but more ambiguous, area.
   (a) Managers' perceptions of the opportunities for choice will be greater in organizations that are divided into small separate units, or clearly defined departments.
   (b) A matrix organization increases managers' sense of constraints and with it reduces their awareness of opportunities for choice.
2. Some organizations offer more opportunities for developing personal expertise than others.
   (a) Opportunities are likely to be greater in organizations with an organic system of management.
3. The opportunities for developing personal domains will differ markedly between organizations.
   (a) This is likely to be influenced most by the attitude of top management to such activities.

A brief comment should be made about the information that suggested these propositions. Propositions 1, 1(a), and 1(b) come from the third study listed in Appendix 1 and from discussions during the exercises on choice at managerial courses. Marshall and Stewart (1981b) described how the managers that they studied differed both in their percentage estimates of the amount of choice that they had in their jobs and in the kinds of choices that they described. To some of those studied, opportunities for choice meant having a well defined area of discretion. This was true for production superintendents in a paper and packaging plant. We also found retail chain store managers who saw themselves as having considerable opportunities for choice, even though they had to operate within highly formalized head office policies. By contrast, many of the managers in a large chemical works complained of constraints, although the company permitted, even encouraged, the development of personal domains. A larger more ambiguous area for choice may be seen more in terms of constraints than of choices because the exercise of many of the choices is dependent upon, or felt to be dependent upon, getting the cooperation of other people.

Propositions 2, 2(a), 3, and 3(a) stem partly from comparisons between marketing and financial jobs at different levels in two large manufacturing companies: one in the chemical industry, the other in electronics. There were more opportunities for developing personal domains in the chemical company. Participation in working parties, in university recruiting and other external activities was generally encouraged, whereas managers in the electronics company were usually expected to restrict their energies to their own responsibilities. However, the latter had greater opportunities to develop an area of personal expertise. The system of management in the two functions was more organic in the electronics than in the chemical company. Another of the companies included in the third research project, which offered choices of personal expertise in many of the jobs studied, was a travel company. This company was also characterized by an organic system of management. One would expect proposition 2(a) to be true, as Burns and Stalker (1961) give, as a characteristic of the organic form of organization, 'the contributive nature of special knowledge and expertise to the common task of the concern' (p. 121).

Boundary roles

There is considerable interest, particularly in the USA, in research into boundary roles; in exploring the functions that involve boundary-spanning and the contributions that can be made by boundary roles, and in discussing the problems that such roles present to their holders. These studies have treated boundary-spanning outside the organization as a distinctive role, with particular problems of trying to work with the different expectations and attitudes of people in one's own organization and outside. People in these roles are contrasted with those who have purely internal roles (Miles, 1980). However, in the large chemical company that we studied in the third research project most of the middle and senior managers had to have, or chose to have, some external contacts. (We do not have sufficient information about the

101

junior managers.) Boundary-spanning in that organization was common; purely internal jobs were rare, and where they existed could reflect the individual's choice.

The framework of demands, constraints, and choices can offer another way of looking at boundary roles: at how far they are a demand of the job, what constraints there are upon individuals wishing to perform such roles, and the kinds of choices that exist in particular organizations for individuals to do so. The difference, cited earlier, between the chemical and the electronics company suggests that it may be worth exploring the extent to which top management permits or encourages its management to participate in boundary-spanning activities, and the effects of doing this upon the individuals' interest in their work and upon particular aspects of organizational effectiveness. Does, for example, the prevalence of boundary-spanning among managers in an organization lead to lower stress than in organizations where boundary-spanning outside the organization is a more specialized role?

Summary

This chapter has put forward a variety of suggestions for teaching and research. There are four broad themes underlying this diverse collection. The first, and our main thesis, is that the extent and variety of the opportunities for choice that exist in managerial jobs—that is, their flexibility—has important implications for the way we should look at jobs, whether as a teacher, researcher, or job analyst. The second is the need for greater care in research design in studying managerial attitudes, managerial behaviour, and managerial work, both in seeking to compare like with like before we attempt to draw any conclusions, and in being clear whether our information is about perceptions, behaviour, or jobs. The third is that we should seek to increase our understanding of the nature, variety, origins, and implications of managerial behaviour; the implications are for selection, training, appraisal, career design, and effectiveness. The fourth is the plea for more people to take an interest in the development of new concepts for understanding managerial work and behaviour.

11.

Implications for the individual manager

This chapter aims to help individual managers and administrators to become more effective and to enjoy their work more. It is about enjoyment as well as effectiveness, because the framework of demands, constraints, and choices can be used for either or both. The suggestions that are made are based on the many courses that we have run to help managers to stand back and take a fresh look at their jobs and at the way that they do them. The aim is to help readers to review how well they understand their jobs and to recognize more clearly what is distinctive about the way that they do them. In Appendix 3 we give various exercises that managers on the courses found helpful.

How well do you understand your job?

Individuals see their jobs very differently, as we saw in Chapter 8. This means that one's view of one's job is likely to be idiosyncratic. To check on one's effectiveness, one needs to recognize what is distinctive about how one sees the job and about how one does it. Understanding the first is an essential prerequisite for appreciating the second. It is not easy to do either, because many managers find it hard to stand back and look at their job or themselves from the outside.

The framework of demands, constraints, and choices offers a good way of helping managers to take a more objective look at their job because it enables them to look at it from a different perspective. Many managers find that they tend to exaggerate the amount of their time that is mortgaged by demands, that is, by work that they must do. They see as demands work that another jobholder may treat as a choice. One reason for this is that they vary in the importance that they attach to the expectations of the different people with whom they work. Individuals also differ considerably, as we saw in Chapter 8, in their view of constraints, but it seems to be more common to exaggerate them than to be able to see them correctly. The evidence for this tendency to exaggerate demands and constraints, and thus to restrict the opportunities for choice, comes from the courses where managers were asked in small groups to review the jobs of one member in terms of demands, constraints, and choices.

Usually the other members both pointed out the areas where the individual saw as a demand or a constraint something that they thought was a choice, and also had their viewpoint accepted by him. They were in consequence able to suggest various opportunities for choice that the individual had not previously recognized but now wished to explore.

There are three ways, our research and course work suggest, by which managers may reduce their perception of the choices available. One is by exaggerating demands, so that they feel that all, or almost all, their time is prescribed. Another is by exaggerating the constraints, so that they think that they are not able to do things that are possible. Yet another is by tunnel vision, resulting from the tendency to focus attention on particular aspects of the job. An unnecessarily restricted view of opportunities for choice can make for a more secure and easier work life, but also one that may be both less effective and duller than with a more accurate perception of the scope of the job.

Reviewing your approach

We suggested in Chapter 8 that most of the managers we studied were usually too busy doing the job in the way that came most naturally to them to review how they did it. This chapter argues, from the evidence of working with managers on courses and individually, that those who are willing to review how they see and do their job can find this useful.

Individuals do jobs differently. We know it, but rarely use this information to consider how someone else might do one's job. It may be argued that our differences in personality and abilities naturally make us do our jobs differently, so that it is not relevant for an individual to consider how someone else might see and do the job. However, attempting to look at the job from the outside can give one a better picture of what it is like. Thinking about how someone else might do the job is a way of trying to do this. Another is thinking about how you could describe the job to your successor. We describe below some factors that can help in considering what is distinctive about your approach to your job.

Beliefs about managing

Managers tend to develop beliefs about the way that they should manage, which they bring with them to any new job. Some may be seen as imperatives, that is, things that must be done or not done. We described some of these in Chapter 8. They may be in the form, 'any manager should' or 'I should' or 'The right way to manage is . . .'. Generally, one is more aware of some of one's own beliefs than of others'. It helps in understanding your distinctive approach to the job to recognize what your beliefs about managing are and how they affect your view of demands, constraints, and choices. There will be certain things

104

that are personal demands because you believe that it is right to do them. Beliefs may also impose personal constraints upon actions.

Guidelines for managing

Beliefs about how to manage are more important for some managers than for others, who may take a primarily pragmatic approach, though that in itself also reflects a belief. In addition to beliefs, managers develop their own ways of tackling jobs. For some these are explicit and can be called strategies for tackling any job. We saw examples in Chapter 8. Others have a more implicit approach. The latter can find it helpful to try and identify what guidelines they use in practice so as to review their current utility.

Personal priorities or agenda

Beliefs and guidelines help to determine how one approaches a job; so do one's own objectives. Discussions with managers, both during the different studies and on courses, show that many do not realize that there is a distinction between the formal objectives and their own. Yet this distinction can help to explain why managers in similar jobs may do different kinds of work. It was often easier for other managers on the courses to identify an individual's personal priorities than it was for the individual to do so, unless he or she was one of the small minority who had a definite strategy for doing the job.

Kotter and Lawrence (1974) used the word 'agenda' to describe the personal objectives of the mayors that they studied. Kotter (1982) described how the agendas of the 15 general managers (GMs) whom he studied in the USA differed from the formal ones:

Although all except one of the organizations involved had a formal planning process which produced written plans, the GMs' organizational agendas always included goals, priorities, strategies, and plans that were not in the written documents. This is not to say that the formal plans and the GMs' organizational agendas were incompatible. Generally, they were very consistent. They were just different. The formal plans tended to be mostly written in terms of detailed numbers. The GMs' organizational agendas tended to be less detailed in numerical objectives, and more detailed in some strategies and plans. They also tended to be less clear, explicit, and logical.

[manuscript, Chapter 4, p. 3]

The value of recognizing your personal objectives, that is, the agenda that you pursue in practice, is that by making them explicit you can check to see whether the objectives are those that you really most want to pursue. it is essential to recognize that in seeking to describe your personal objectives you should not just repeat the formal objectives—an exercise to help you to identify

105

your own is given in Appendix 3 (exercise 8). Someone else might list the same formal objectives but do the job differently—radically differently, if it is a job that offers a wide choice of domain.

Recognizing your focuses of attention

Individuals will tend to emphasize some parts of the job more than others, as we saw in Chapter 2, on 'Common choices'. One manager will, for example, pay more attention to the technical aspects of the job, another to supervision or administration. To have a realistic picture of the demands of the job and the opportunities for choice that it offers, you need to recognize your focuses of attention.

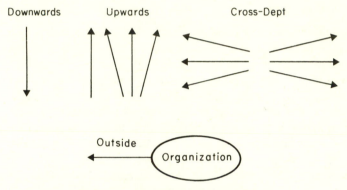

Fig. 11.1   In which directions are you focused?

An easy way of doing this is to look at how your time is distributed between different categories of contacts. Figure 11.1 illustrates the different directions in which attention may be focused: downwards, upwards, sideways, and outwards. Not all jobs offer all these choices, but most offer some choice between the time spent with subordinates or with people in other departments. Our research has shown that people in similar jobs can divide their time very differently between their contacts. The opportunities for such choice in similar jobs was illustrated in Chapter 2, Table 2.1, which showed how two plant managers divided their time very differently between subordinates and people in other departments.

Various diary-keeping studies have shown that managers do not necessarily have a correct idea of how they spend their time. It can therefore be useful to keep a diary of how you spend your time for at least a week, preferably longer. This can help you to check whether you divide your time between different aspects of the job, and different people, in the way that you imagine. A diary form is illustrated in Appendix 3.

106

Taking a strategic view

The word 'strategy' figured importantly in Chapters 4 and 5, where we discussed what kinds of job permit their holders to do widely different kinds of work. Such jobs have flexible domains: we distinguished between those that offered some choice in the nature of the work that could be done by the unit for which the manager was responsible, and those that offered a choice of personal domain outside the unit. We argued that in jobs with a flexible domain managers are likely to be more effective if they take a strategic view of what they can do. This is the individual version of a top management group who are advised by consultants to decide what business they are in, and to do this by reviewing the organization's assets, including what its people are good at doing, and the nature of the competition and the environment.

Managers who are in, or about to be moved to, jobs with flexible domains should be able to enhance their effectiveness by considering the following points:

– What opportunities exist for changing the nature of the unit's work?
– What kind of advantages and disadvantages are likely to be associated with any such change?
– What role can you most usefully play in furthering the effectiveness of the unit? To answer this means taking into account the nature of the tasks to be done, both within the unit and outside it, and the contribution that you can best make. The latter means considering your own strengths and weaknesses compared with those of subordinates as well as the desirability of staff development. It means, too, recognizing what work you can more easily do because of your more senior position.
– What work needs to be done at the boundary of the unit (see Chapter 3) to protect it from disturbance and/or to make it easier to change? This may need to include trying to manage your boss.
– What other work can or should you be doing that is not directly related to the unit? How important is this compared with work for the unit? What criteria should be used to judge importance?
– What contribution can you make to the effectiveness of the larger unit of which your own forms a part?
– How does your contribution fit in with that which is being made, or could be made by others?
– What is the best, and what is the worst, that could happen by stopping doing something that one is currently doing? by doing something different?

This is not meant to be a complete checklist, or a list for the successful management of change, as the latter is adequately considered in other books. It is given to show some of the questions that the manager who takes a strategic view should be asking.

107

It is useful to consider the possibilities first, as if there were no constraints, and only then, like the manager quoted at the start of Chapter 8, to examine the constraints. A strategic view will necessarily include considering what constraints may restrict or prevent what the manager wants to do and whether, and if so how, they can be overcome. Many managers are pretty adept at thinking of ways round policies and procedures that they dislike, but are often less proactive and inventive about overcoming other constraints. One of the most important of these is usually the reactions of other people, so that we should now consider the choices that the manager may have in developing a supportive network of contacts.

Developing and managing your network

Managers need to think politically, and the more senior the manager and the more flexible the domain the more necessary this is. Some people do this instinctively; many, if they are to rise above the specialist ranks, learn to do so; but probably most could improve their skill, and some junior and middle managers do not recognize the need. Even of those who are skilful, few take a strategic view of their network of contacts. Mintzberg (1973) and Kotter and Lawrence (1974) both drew attention to the importance of the manager's contacts with other departments or outside the organization. Mintzberg described 'liaison' contacts 'to gain favours and information' as one of the ten managerial roles that he identified. Sayles (1964) gave the most extended and searching account of the importance of the manager's network of contacts:

The one enduring objective of the manager is the effort to build and maintain a predictable, reciprocating system of relationships. . . .[1]

It should be, but in our experience it is not often recognized as an objective. It may be that British managers tend to be less conscious of this objective than the American managers about whom Mintzberg and Sayles were writing.

An exercise is suggested in Appendix 3 (number 9) to help managers to think more strategically about their network of contacts. Some of the questions that a manager can usefully consider for the development and management of a network of contacts are as follows.

– Who is in my network? That is, whom do I know well enough to ask for information or favours?
– Who is not there whom it would be useful to have within it?
– How effective are each of those contacts for getting the information and support that I may need?
– What can be done to strengthen a relationship and/or develop a new one?

1. From Sayles, L. R., *Managerial Behaviour*, © 1964. McGraw-Hill Book Company, New York, p. 258.

108

– Who might want to help in supporting a specific plan?
– What price may I have to pay for seeking help? Have I overdrawn the balance of goodwill?
– What kind of exchange does each member of the network value?
– What exchanges, trades, have I got to offer a particular contact?

Some people may think that this is too cold-blooded, even an immoral, way of looking at relationships. Yet management does mean achieving objectives with, and by means of, other people. Those who are not instinctive politicians should consider how they can become more effective at developing a 'reciprocating system of relationships', in Sayles's phrase. Put like that, it sounds more moral. Whether it is or not—and there is no sharp line separating the ethical and unethical—depends both upon the ends and upon what means are used.

Different stages in a job

A strategic view of one's job should include taking into account the opportunities that may exist at different periods in it. It is particularly important to try and develop a strategy in the first few months, so as not unthinkingly to restrict future opportunities for choice. It is easy to establish expectations of what you will do. These may become demands that are later difficult to change.

Being in a job some time is likely to affect the available choices. Your actions will have closed off or restricted some of the potential choices, but it is worth considering what new opportunities for choice have developed. These can come from learning how to get things done, including who is likely to be helpful and whom it is desirable to try and circumvent. There should also be more time to exploit some of the choices. There may be less need to spend time in supervision, so that more attention can be given to other aspects of the job. Opportunities for choice may be recognized that were not evident at the start of the job. This can be true, for example, of the choice to develop a special expertise in some aspect of the job. Periodic reviews of your strategy should be made to check both on how the previous strategy is working out, and also to identify new opportunities for choice.

A career strategy?

The query is relevant because some managers, at least in Britain, do not have, and do not wish to have, a strategy for their career. They prefer to take things as they come. This is, for some, a reflection of their philosophy of life; for others, it stems from a belief that they can safely leave decisions about their career to their seniors: promotion will be offered if they work well. The only choice they need make will be whether to accept it. These statements apply to managers in companies that traditionally have offered a lifetime career to their managers; 'traditionally', because a change in the company's fortunes will affect whether or not this remains true. Managers who have to move, or who are interested in doing so, will necessarily take a more active approach.

Attitudes to careers and to whether one should seek to manage them probably reflects cross-cultural differences. Perhaps, as Fowles has said,

There are means-oriented societies for whom the game is the game; and ends-oriented societies, for whom the game is winning. In the first, if one is happy then one is successful; in the second, one cannot be happy unless one is successful.[2]

The evidence of differences in jobs that we have discussed in this book and in its predecessor, *Contrasts in Management* (Stewart, 1976), has implications for those who want to try and plan their careers. The implications from this book are that a career strategy should be based on an understanding of the choices that you want to exercise and of the jobs that will provide them. An understanding of the kinds of constraints that one finds helpful or frustrating is another guideline to thinking about a future career.

These suggestions are in addition to the advice that is offered in numerous books about how to further one's career by playing politics and creating the desired impression. They are additional, too, to the helpful guidelines provided by Schein (1975) in his concept of career anchors as the central aspect of work that matters most to particular individuals, and to the description of different career stages (Schein, 1978). We are emphasizing two further points: first, that individuals can choose, if they wish, to develop a career strategy just as they can choose to review how they approach their job. Some individuals will necessarily be more constrained than others by their age, abilities, and the market for their skills, but most could have a strategy. The other point is that our analysis of demands, constraints, and choices offers another useful way of thinking about the kinds of jobs that are likely to suit one best.

Assessing your effectiveness

A better understanding of the nature and possibilities of your job and of your approach to it can help you to assess your effectiveness. This can be attempted either now or when you have completed the exercises in Appendix 3. The following is suggested as a checklist arising out of the discussion in this and previous chapters.

– Do you have a strategy for your job?
– How much of your week is spent mainly reacting to short-term events?

2. Fowles, J., *The Aristos*, © John Fowles 1964, 1968, 1970, 1980. Cape, London, p. 159.

– When did you last review what you are actually doing and how effective you are?
– What choices are you making in the job? Look at what you focus your attention upon (see exercise 8).
– How well do your choices match the following:
  – What you can best contribute to current needs?
  – What others, your subordinates and colleagues, can best contribute?
– What gaps are left by the choices that you make?
– Are you doing anything to try and ensure that these are filled?
– Are you treating as demands work that you do not have to do? If so, is it more important than other work that you might do?
– What are you not doing that you think should be done?
  – Is this because you don't have time? If so, keep a diary and review both the appropriateness of what you are spending your time on, and the efficiency with which you organize your time.
  – Is this because you feel too constrained? If so, try discussing with someone else the nature of these constraints and ways that they might be overcome.
– Have you built a 'reciprocating system of relationships', in Sayles's phrase? That is, how good is your network? Does it support you well in what you are doing now? Will it support changes that you may want to make? (see exercise 9).
– Are you enjoying your work? Do you feel full of energy?

This checklist obviously does not cover all the questions that you could ask yourself about your effectiveness. It is limited to topics arising from our research and courses. The main omissions are questions about how you judge the output of your work and that of your unit. In some jobs this is easy to do, in others it is difficult. Another important omission is questions about your effectiveness as a supervisor and developer of others.

Enjoying your job

The last question on the checklist above was about your enjoyment, which will also be reflected in your energy level. If your answers were negative and you are well, you should use the framework of demands, constraints, and choices to explore why you feel like that and whether you have opportunities for choice that would make your work more enjoyable. On some of the courses there were managers who felt shut in and rather bored and frustrated: using the framework, and helped by discussions with other managers or working alone, some of them at least saw opportunities for making their job more interesting—'it has opened doors that I thought were shut twenty years ago'. That is a true but untypical statement, yet even modest changes in the way that one views one's job and the possibilities for choice in it can help to make work more enjoyable.

12.

Implications for the organization

This book was written in the belief that we need an improved way of analysing managerial jobs, of understanding the differences between them, and of taking into account what managers actually do: a way that can be used both by those who have to take decisions about managers and about their jobs and by individual managers in thinking about their work and careers. This chapter will review the implications for the organization of our researches, and of the framework of demands, constraints, and choices on which they were based. It will start by looking at what an organization needs to know about its jobs and its managers, and at the criteria that can be used to assess how effectively the organization uses its managers. The implications of the previous chapters will be discussed for each of the following: management philosophy, organizational structure, selection, and appraisals. Management development was discussed in Chapter 10. We shall conclude with suggestions for action.

What the organization needs to know about a job

The term 'organization' is used, as it was in the preface, for all those who have to take decisions about managers and about managerial jobs. This includes senior management, personnel and training managers, organizational specialists, and all managers in their supervisory capacity. The knowledge that is needed about a particular job can be summarized as follows.

1. Why is it necessary? What is/are the output(s) expected from it?
2. What, if any, trade-offs of outcome are acceptable? What are the most important outcomes at the present time?
3. What are its responsibilities? What is the scale of the job?
4. To what extent can it be considered on its own as distinct from part of a pair or a group of jobs?
5. Has the job changed recently? What changes are currently taking place and what ones are likely?
6. How flexible is it; that is, what are the different kinds of work that can be done?
7. What kinds of skills, abilities, and knowledge does it require?

8. How can performance be assessed?
9. What is the appropriate salary for the job?
10. What kinds of experience and development does it offer?

This list was developed by considering what our researches had to add to understanding the information that is needed in an organization to make appropriate decisions about managerial jobs. The aim was to list the points in a logical order, starting with the need for the job and moving through the information required to answer subsequent questions. The second point is in its logical position, but its significance is explained by the sixth. Many of the questions will be familiar to the personnel reader. The first is a familiar one, even though it may not be reviewed as often as it should be. In some organizations the answer will be more straightforward than in others and hence less in need of review. The third, seventh, eighth, ninth, and tenth points are common considerations in personnel management, and the fifth is also familiar though less often asked. The remaining questions—two, four, and six—are ones whose importance has been highlighted by the research, and to answering which the research can make a contribution. It can also do so, as we shall see later in this chapter, to most of the others.

What the organization needs to know about a potential jobholder

The information required can be summarized as:

1. How well is this individual likely to do the job? What will be his or her strengths and weaknesses in it?
2. What aspects of the job will be emphasized and developed? Which ones may be ignored?
3. What is similar and what is different in this job to those that the person has had before?
4. What training may be needed for the aspects of the job that are new to this person?
5. What can this individual contribute to the group(s) to which he or she will belong? How well does this contribution fit in with those of other members?
6. What support may this individual need to contribute maximally?
7. What part can this job play in this individual's development?

This list was developed in the same way as the previous one.

The first question is the essential one that all selectors must ask themselves, and the third will commonly be asked. The fourth and the sixth may be asked, but even so may not get the attention that they merit. The seventh may be asked only about those who are considered to be high-fliers. The importance of the other questions, the second and the fifth, has been shown by the research described in earlier chapters. They take account of the flexibility in a job, the fact that individuals will focus their attention upon different aspects of it. They also take into account the opportunity that may exist for work-sharing.

Criteria for assessing the organization's effectiveness in its use of managers

Readers may find the following criteria a useful way of reviewing how satisfied they are with the organization's use of its managers. The criteria are suggested as guidelines based upon the lessons of the research and of the courses on managerial work. We start with managers rather than jobs because they are more important to an organization's effectiveness.

An effective organization will have managers who:

– Are suited to the jobs that need to be done
– Have the energy and the interest to explore ways of doing them better
– Believe that it is possible to make changes
– Accept the constraints as reasonable, but are not uncritical of them
– Know what is expected from them
– Know how they are matching up to these expectations
– Feel that they have an area of responsibility where they can take decisions

An effective organization will seek to match people to jobs so that:

– As far as possible, people do work that they enjoy and so contribute the extra energy that comes from that
– The individual's strengths are matched to the current needs of the job, including, where this is relevant, the ability to think strategically
– The individual's focuses of attention are those that are needed at the time
– In pair and team jobs the individual's strengths complement those of the other members
– Those in jobs with very defined tasks have some additional task that offers more scope for flexibility and hence for choice
– When people are moved to another job it provides some stimulus that is different from the previous one, so that they are encouraged to review their habits of managing, and have the opportunity to learn new skills.

Readers' views of the appropriateness of these criteria will depend upon their philosophy of management, so we shall start our discussion by looking at the implications for that.

Implications for management philosophy

Some readers may be shocked at the amount of choice that has been described in earlier chapters and at some of the quotations from managers. An effective

115

organization, they may think, is one where people both know what should be done and do it. Given the variability of human beings, there will necessarily be some choice of style, but they may think that there should not be a choice in what work is done. Senior management can obviously seek to, and to some extent must try to, restrict certain kinds of choice. It will usually do so both formally and informally—formally by policies and procedures, and informally by the climate it seeks to create to guide managers' behaviour. However, even in the most controlled organization opportunities for choice remain.

The problem is to make good use of this fact, rather than to try to pretend that it can be prevented, or to believe that it does not exist. There is a difference between establishing objectives and priorities so that managers know what they should be aiming for, and trying to make people concentrate upon work that is not what they would naturally choose to do. The horticultural analogy is relevant; while many different kinds of plants can be grown in the same garden, some will grow well in some parts of it but not in others, and some will not grow at all. It is better to find the plant that is suited to the conditions, or else to try, though that is harder, to adapt the conditions to the plant. But first one must understand both the conditions of the garden and the preferences of the plant. Some plants are more adaptable than others, but some of the finest are the most choosy about the conditions in which they will give of their best. The analogy, like most analogies, is not a perfect one, but it is a useful guide to the management philosophy that our research suggests is most likely to meet the criteria suggested above.

The gardener, that is, top management, has a choice in the kind of plants selected, in changing some of the conditions in which they grow, and in seeking to curtail their height and breadth; but there are limits, as any gardener knows, to what can be done. There are also surprises, as some plants succeed unexpectedly well in conditions that are not supposed to suit them. There is a temptation, to which many gardeners succumb, of seeing a fine plant and thinking that one must have it, even though one's conditions may not be right for it. Good gardeners will learn what plants suit the garden, how different parts of the garden suit different plants, what can be done to improve growing conditions, the need to stop some plants smothering others, and also what plants they prefer. They will know, too, the constraints that they can modify and those that they cannot change.

There are choices to be made in the organization about the kind of managers that are wanted, and about what distinctions should be made in that. Should all managers be encouraged to look for possibilities of change and expansion in their responsibilities? Or is this desirable in only a few high-fliers? Or only in some kinds of job? These are the kind of questions that ought to be being asked within the organization. Decisions will be made about them, though they may not be explicit.

The organization needs to know what kind of managers it really wants. It is so easy to fool oneself, to believe that one wants managers with plenty of initiative but to provide jobs that offer no choice of domain; to believe that the most important thing is to have managers who are good at supervision, but to put them in positions where what they most need are the political skills to enlist support and cooperation from peers and bosses. An understanding of what one's management philosophy is in practice, as distinct from theory, can help one to get a better match between the individual manager and the nature of the job, which includes the organizational setting and climate.

We found considerable differences between organizations in how managers talk about their opportunities to exercise choice. One manager commented:

I believe that in our company the idea that the individual has far more freedom than he thinks is deliberately fostered. No one is afraid of people taking on responsibility. So if you want to take responsibility it's there. How much freedom you have depends upon how much you are willing to take.

While not all managers that we interviewed in that company, which was a manufacturer of paper packing, thought like that, it was a more common view there than we found elsewhere. Managers in some organizations are necessarily more interdependent than those in others. The constraints that come from such interdependence will make it hard to give managers the feeling expressed in the quotation above. Yet even within these constraints there will be differences of management philosophy that will influence whether managers are more conscious of constraints, of demands, or of opportunities for choice.

The opportunities to exercise choice, and managers' perceptions of them, will be affected by the philosophy of senior management; so will the kind of demands and the time that they absorb. The demands may be increased in a number of ways that stem from different philosophies: from the institution of many bureaucratic procedures that cannot be delegated; from the importance attached to consultation or to managers being always available; and from the expectation that managers should be able to answer detailed questions about the operation of their units.

One organizational policy or practice that has repercussions on the range of choice that jobs offer is whether managers are permitted or encouraged to make work contacts outside the organization. One policy is to make such contacts only the task of the relevant specialist. This makes for clear channels of communication and for concentration upon one's defined responsibilities and for use of specialist knowledge. An alternative policy is to permit or encourage managers generally to share in the task of building contacts in the community, and to make contacts outside the organization that are relevant to their work, so that the works manager, for example, can get to know suppliers and customers. Such a policy has the advantage of establishing more links

117

with the outside world, of enabling managers to do their own boundary management (see Chapter 3) making it easier for them to develop special expertise (Chapter 7), and generally giving them a wider choice of activities and a better understanding of the organization's environment. The nature of the business and the management philosophy will help to determine which policy or practice is adopted, but the existence of the choice should be recognized and the possibilities evaluated.

Implications for organizational structure

We know remarkably little about what a job's worth of work is at the managerial level. The traditional answer was that it was determined by the span of control; but the very wide diversity of spans that exist in practice, and the various reasons why this can be appropriate, have made that guideline of very limited help. The evidence that we have provided of the great flexibility that exists in some jobs, particularly the more senior ones, should help to renew interest in considering which jobs are really necessary and why. However, the fact that a job has a flexible domain should not be taken as an indication that it may be unnecessary, or that one that has a fixed domain will be necessary because some well defined work may not need doing. Our research cannot tell us when a job is necessary, but it highlights the desirability of paying more attention to considering that. Organizations need to steer between having too few jobs, so that the work that must be done gets most of the attention and the work that is a choice, though it may be very important, gets too little, and having too many jobs, so that individuals either create unnecessary work and systems for others or spend their time pursuing domains that are of only marginal utility to the organization.

The framework of demands, constraints, and choices can contribute to a better understanding of the kinds of managerial jobs that there are in the organization. It can also help in a review of their design. One recommendation suggested by Chapter 8 on how managers see choice is to try and provide managers with a clear area of responsibility where they can feel free to take initiatives. This was the characteristic of a job that was most often mentioned as giving choice. Some kinds of businesses can more easily do so than others, and in some the need to consider industrial relations' repercussions elsewhere can act as a frustrating constraint. Even in the most interdependent organizations there may be some scope for trying to provide managers with an area of their own or a refreshing change to a job that does offer more scope, which need not necessarily be a more senior one.

We have shown that jobs differ in their flexibility, that is in the range and kinds of choice that they offer. One implication of this is to consider, as some managements do, how much flexibility a job offers. In the more constrained jobs, such as financial accounting, it may be desirable to include some task that is more open-ended, to stimulate the individual to think about what should be done and to provide the satisfaction that some people will get from greater variety.

One implication of our research is the need to be clear when it is appropriate to think of *a* job, and when one must take into account the other jobholders with whom work may be shared. The sharing that can take place in teams and in pair jobs needs recognition in thinking both of the relative strengths and weaknesses of the members and of the kind of work they choose to do. We need to recognize, too, that in some organizations a jobholder may be a member of several teams. In Chaper 6 we considered the organizational implications of work-sharing in more detail.

Implications for selection

What the framework of demands, constraints, and choices can contribute to selection is another way of thinking about the match between the manager and the job. A good match is one where the demands are competently fulfilled, but since these are often a small part of the job, it is even more important that the manager's likely choices should be those that are needed. It is helpful here to try and get as much information as possible about the individual's focuses of attention. Drucker (1967), in *The Effective Executive*, suggested that one should seek to build on a manager's strengths. What we are suggesting is somewhat different, though not incompatible with his advice, and that is to try and give managers jobs where the choices that they are likely to want to exercise will be those that are needed in the job at that time. Schein's (1975) concept of career anchors, where he argues that individuals develop their views of the aspects of work that are most important to them, is another way of thinking about and recognizing an individual's focuses of attention.

The most important implication for selection of the opportunities for choice in jobs is the need to describe them more realistically. It seems a pity, when so much effort is spent on job descriptions, that managers usually find them irrelevant when they are in the job. Even as a guide for selection they are inadequate: they only give some of the information that one needs about a job; they provide a formal and rather idealized picture, which is only a partial guide to what the job is actually like. We need much of the information that is contained in the better job descriptions, such as the scope of the job, the key tasks, and its organizational setting, but we need, too, a description of the nature of the flexibility in the job, that is, the demands and constraints that define its choices, and what is distinctive about those choices. This framework was used to describe the job of the district administrator in the National Health Service in the fourth research study but, as that is a rather unusual kind of job, Appendix 2 illustrates how demands, constraints, and choices can be used to add to the official job description of two other jobs.

119

Implications for appraisals

There is often more concern about the effectiveness of the design and operation of appraisals, whether they are of performance or of potential, than about other personnel procedures. One of the difficulties is deciding what to appraise, given the problems of designing a good form and the reluctance of many appraisers to be frank either on a form or in discussions with the appraisee. An even greater difficulty for many managers is conducting an appraisal interview that both parties feel has been worthwhile. There are problems, too, in assessing an individual's potential for promotion. Often this is done in very general terms, such as whether the individual is ready for promotion or to what level he or she is likely to be promotable. Such a broad approach to planning management succession can still leave gaps when there are senior vacancies, because the needs of the job do not match the abilities of the individuals available.

Demands, constraints, and choices can make a contribution to appraisal interviews by providing a way of exploring what an individual does in a job. A discussion of the current demands of the job, its constraints and opportunities for choice can help to show what the job is currently like (bosses can often be out-of-date, or unrealistic about this), how the individual sees the job, what work the individual is currently focusing his or her attention upon, and whether this is the most appropriate for current needs. Such an approach can lead to a better mutual understanding and evaluation of what is being done, why it is being done, and whether that is what is needed. However, the framework of demands, constraints, and choices does not have anything to contribute to the assessment of how well it is done, as distinct from an assessment of what is being done.

A discussion of the demands of the job should include a review of the jobholder's perception of demands. The individual may treat as demand work that the boss thinks is not vital, or see as a choice something that the boss thinks must be done. A joint understanding of both these points of view, and of the reasons for them, can help to ensure that the jobholder knows what the boss sees to be the demand core of the job. A review of the jobholder's perception of constraints can be particularly helpful for encouraging those who have an exaggerated idea of them to recognize that they have more scope than they think. A discussion of constraints can also tell the boss what he or she is contributing to this feeling of excessive constraint. A review of the opportunities for choice in the job can be used as a means of exploring the appropriateness of the choices that the jobholder is currently taking. It can also be used to help the jobholder to take a more strategic view of the job: of what needs doing, of what are the possibilities and which ones should be developed in the following year. These suggestions highlight the important role that the boss can play as a coach. We discussed in the chapter under training implications the importance of identifying and making full use of the managers who are good coaches.

Managers differ in whether they see their environment as something that they can influence or as being so constraining and/or demanding that they are unable to do so. This difference will be affected by the job and the culture of the organization, but there are also, as various studies have shown, important personality differences. However, it is possible, our course work shows, to help managers to see that they are not as confined as they think. Not all managers will welcome this: we found that some said that they prefer to feel constrained, as more choice would be disturbing.

We found that bosses tended to see the job as bigger, and as providing more opportunities for innovation, than did their subordinates. We did not seek to explore the reasons for this, or how common it is, though it could be useful to do so in another study. There are at least two possible explanations. One is that the boss is better able to take a detached view and to see the scope of the job, while the jobholder is constrained by his or her habits of managing and focuses of attention. Individuals will have their own personal view of demands, constraints, and choices and may not be able to see beyond them. Another possible explanation is that the boss does not have an adequate understanding of the constraints that restrict the jobholder, particularly those created by himself or herself. If the first is at least partially true it has implications for using the appraisal interview to explore the subordinate's view of the scope of the job as an aid to management development. If the second is true, the interview can provide an opportunity for the boss to learn more about the effects of his or her style of management—an opportunity that few may want to take.

We saw in Chapters 4 and 5 that some jobs have flexible domains so that different jobholders can work in different domains. Appraisals of managers in such jobs require an understanding of the domain within which the individual is actually operating, and of the relative importance of other potential domains at that time. Such an assessment is more difficult in jobs that permit of work-sharing, because it needs to take into account how well the individual's activities match those with whom work is shared. Managers who occupy jobs with flexible domains are likely to be more effective if they can think strategically about what work needs doing, and about how their contribution matches those of others. They may need help and stimulus to do so, especially if they have previously held jobs that they have learnt to operate by habit.

One implication of the flexibility in jobs is that appraisals need to pay more attention to what is not being done. An individual's focuses of attention may leave gaps that need filling. This can also be true in a management team.

Conclusions and specific suggestions

The framework of demands, constraints, and choices, and the research that developed and used it, can point to some specific actions that should help to improve managerial effectiveness. These apply to the organization as a whole and to middle and senior managers reviewing their own staff. They are listed below. They summarize suggestions made in this and earlier chapters, so the number of the relevant chapter is given.

1. For decisions about the organization's use of its managers

– Review the criteria for assessing effectiveness in using the organization's managers and consider how well these are being met (this chapter).
– Review what kind of managers are really wanted and what myths may exist about this (Chapter 4 and this chapter). A review of your reactions to the different quotations in the book can be one guide to what you want (Chapter 8 and initial quotations at the start of some chapters).
– Recognize that managerial jobs differ in ways other than function and level and that these differences should be taken into account in training and career development (Chapters 4–7, 9, and 10).
– Distinguish which junior and middle management jobs have flexible domains, and consider the implications of this for selection, coaching, and career development (Chapters 4 and 5).
– In management development, whether on the job coaching, special tasks, or formal training, seek to encourage strategic thinking about the work that should be done for those in jobs with flexible domains.
– Distinguish which jobs offer the incumbent a defined area of responsibility within which he or she will feel able to exercise initiative and which do not. Consider the implications for individual satisfaction and for job rotation (Chapter 8 and this chapter).
– Identify the jobs that require, or permit, work-sharing, and consider the relevance for training and selection (Chapter 6).
– Consider what managerial habits are being formed and how appropriate these are for the current jobs and for subsequent jobs (Chapter 8 and 10).

2. For decisions about individual managerial jobs

– Review how you tell that a job is necessary (this chapter).
– In selection, use demands, constraints , and choices in addition to the normal job description so as to tell you more about the kind of job that you are filling (Appendix 3 and this chapter).
– In selection for a flexible job, consider what domains you want to be used (Chapters 4, 5, and 8).
– Consider which are the more constrained jobs and whether some more open-ended task should be added to them (this chapter).

122

3. For decisions about the selection, appraisal, training, and development of individual managers and members of management teams

- In appraisal interviews, use demands, constraints, and choices as the way of reviewing what work needs to be done and what the jobholder is doing. Try to help those individuals who have an excessive view of demands or constraints (Chapter 11 and this chapter).
- For managers in reviewing their immediate subordinates, consider what aspects of their jobs are getting a lot of attention and which are getting little or none (Chapters 2 and 5).
- Consider which individuals need to be encouraged to think about boundary management (Chapter 3).
- For members of management teams, consider what are the focuses of attention and what gaps there may be (Chapter 6).
- Identify the choices that individuals make and consider what use can be made of these. Look especially at choices of expertise and the developments that they may make possible (Chapters 2 and 7).
- In selection, collect as much information as you can about the focuses of attention that the individuals being considered have shown in previous jobs; consider the relevance of the choices that the individual is likely to take to current needs in the job (Chapter 8 and this chapter).
- Consider who seems to be lacking in, or running out of, energy and whether some change of job, or some outside task, could be a useful stimulus (Chapter 8 and this chapter).

The framework of demands, constraints, and choices is primarily useful as a way of thinking about the nature of managerial jobs and about how managers do them. It can provide a more realistic understanding of both than can be obtained from the traditional ways of describing jobs, or of thinking about managerial performance, as these tend to be too formal and idealistic. They do not take into account how human beings in jobs actually behave, as was vividly described by Lord Armstrong in the quotation at the start of Chapter 1. A more realistic understanding of behaviour can make for better decisions about how the organization should select, appraise, and develop the managers that it needs, and for a better appreciation of the kind of managers that it really wants.

Appendix 1
The research background to the book

Researchers differ in the nature of the methodological problems with which they are concerned. A major dichotomy is recognized between qualitative and quantitative research which reflects the relative importance that is attached to validity compared with reliability; to conceptual development or reliable measurement, to hypothesis-generating or hypothesis-testing. The studies on which this book is based belong to the qualitative tradition. The prime concern of the qualitative researcher is to try and understand the nature of the subject being studied and to develop fresh insights into what should be studied. Such understanding is an evolving activity that goes through several stages. It may be worth describing, for those who are not experienced researchers, the stages of the research process used for the two main studies on which this book is based, 'A Classification of Choices in Managerial Jobs' and 'The Job and Role of the District Administrator', and for their predecessor 'A Behavioural Classification of Managerial Jobs'.

1. Trying to identify more clearly what was to be studied. Although this is an essential prerequisite for any research application, it is a process that continues to be important, particularly at the pilot stage. One of the characteristics of qualitative research is that the research process may lead to a redefinition of what is being studied, through a recognition of the inadequacies of the original definition.
2. Exploring different ways of studying the subject by considering and testing different methods. This stage should provide further insight into the nature of the subject to be studied as well as into the limitations of the method(s) chosen.
3. The main part of the study, which included an extensive and intensive stage, though in reverse order in the two studies.
4. Preliminary analysis as planned in the earlier stages of the research.
5. A rather lengthy process of reflection upon and judgement of the material collected, during which further concepts were developed, discussed, and assessed and other forms of analysis were tried. The assessment at this stage was in part a personal one: do I think that my understanding of the subject has developed? can this understanding be used? 'used' to work with managers in a way that they find helpful? 'used' to describe the studies and their significance to other academics?

A synopsis of the methods used in the five studies that the author has carried out or supervised over the last 15 years is given in Table A1.1. The discussion of methods here will be limited to numbers 3 and 4 in the table, because the methods used in the others have been discussed elsewhere (Stewart, 1967; Stewart, 1976; Marshall and Stewart, 1981). Similar methods were used in both studies: lengthy interviews with the jobholder using a questionnaire that asked about the job, and observations of managers in comparable jobs. These methods were supplemented in the 'Classification of Choices' study by interviews with the jobholder's boss and by discussions with managers on courses using the model of demands, constraints, and choices to study their jobs, and in the district administrators' study by postal questionnaires on meetings attended, contacts, and the characteristics of the district filled in before the interview and by group discussions. In both studies the design of the interview schedule was aimed at overcoming, as far as possible, the difficulties that some managers have in describing either their job or what they do by concentrating the questions upon the work that had to be or could be done for different aspects of the job.

Methods used in a classification of choices in managerial jobs (Research no. 3 in Table A1.1)

This two-and-a-half year study started from the framework of demands, constraints, and choices developed in the previous study. The aim was to describe the nature of the choices available in managerial jobs and to distinguish how these differed between jobs. An important problem at the first stage was to determine what choices to study, and at the second to discover the best means of identifying the nature of the choices in particular jobs. It was decided that the main emphasis should be on choices in what work was done, rather than on how or with whom it was done because the author's previous studies had concentrated on the pattern of work and relationships rather than on work content and output.

The first stage of the research

An initial approach to trying to decide what choices to study was to ask managers about the choices that they saw in their jobs. This approach was of limited value because, as the research on perceptions of choices later showed, few of the managers studied thought analytically about their jobs in terms of the options or choices open to them. The other approach was to observe six pairs of managers, each pair in a similar job, in six jobs chosen to cover a variety of different kinds of middle management jobs: production, sales, personnel, and service jobs in industry and maintenance, and planning in local government. Each manager was observed for a week and he or she and their

Title of project	Date and duration	Staffing	Nature and size of sample	Methods used
1. Similarities and Differences in How Managers Spend Their Time (Stewart, 1967)	1964–6 2 years		160 middle and senior managers mainly in production, marketing, and accounting in different manufacturing companies	Diary for four weeks covering when, how, where, with whom
2. A Behavioural Classification of Managerial Jobs (Stewart, 1976)	1973–5 $2\frac{1}{2}$ years	1 research worker full-time 2 years (Judy Slinn); 1 full-time 1 year (Richard Turton)	260 managers in jobs selected for diversity of level and function in different companies; 16 managers chosen to represent different contact types	Lengthy questionnaire interviews; Interviews, diaries, observations
3. A Classification of Choices in Managerial Jobs	1977–80 $2\frac{1}{2}$ years	1 research worker full-time 2 years (Phil Long)	98 managers and bosses cross-section by level and function in one company; varied functions in others; 6 pairs of managers in six different jobs	Lengthy open-ended interviews with managers and with their bosses; One week's observation of each manager comparing behaviour of each pair
4. The Job and Role of the District Administrator in the National Health Service (Stewart, Smith, Blake and Wingate, 1980)	1978–9 10 months	3 part-time research associates (Peter Smith, Jenny Blake, and Pauline Wingate)	41 district administrators from a stratified sample of districts	3–7 hour interview; Observation of 11 DAs lasting 3 days to a week each; Group discussions
5. Managers' Perceptions of the Choices in Their Jobs	1978–9 15 months	1 part-time research associate (Judi Marshall)	86 middle managers in production/technical and sales/marketing in three manufacturing companies	Tape-recorded open-ended interviews; Personal background; Job involvement and accommodation questionnaire; Myers–Briggs Tests

Funding: 1: Nuffield Foundation. 2, 3, 5: Social Science Research Council. 4: King Edward's Hospital Fund for London.

127

bosses were interviewed about the job. The purpose of these observations was to try and obtain greater insight into the nature of the demands, constraints, and choices in the jobs. Comparisons were made between each pair to identify the different work that they did and hence the kinds of choices that existed in the job. A description of each job was written in terms of demands, constraints, and choices. One of these descriptions, in a much shortened form, is used as an illustration in Appendix 2.

The observations were made by the research worker, Phil Long, and for one pair of managers by a graduate student with a technical background that was helpful for understanding the work observed. A detailed record was kept on a form provided of where the manager was working, with whom, the form of work, and a synopsis of each activity. The observational record was used to help in determining the questions for the final interview with the jobholder, and for comparing the kind of work that was done by each pair of managers in similar jobs. (The observational method is discussed later.) One of the purposes of the final interview was to try and determine whether the differences in the work observed reflected different choices by the jobholders, different timing of the work done, or differences in the demands and constraints in the situation.

The study of the six pairs of managers suggested that it would be easier to ask about the choices in the job, and to understand their nature, if the job were analysed in systems terms of input, conversion, and output of the work for which the manager was responsible. This enabled one to ask about the demands, constraints, and choices affecting the work at each stage and to find out whether the manager had a choice of determining the nature of the work done by the unit for which he or she was responsible. The other distinction that was found to be helpful was to ask about the different components of the job, and especially what work that the manager did, or could do, within the unit, and what other work had to be done, or could be done, outside the unit.

Interviews in the main study

The development of an interview schedule proved difficult. Different versions of it were tried out in pilot interviews and on courses using the 12 observations as a base. The aim of the different revisions was to try and improve on the understanding of demands, constraints, and choices that could be obtained from the interview. One problem throughout this study, and the other studies, is that many managers do not think analytically about their jobs, and even those that do are likely to have only a partial view of the job. Someone else in the job might, and often does, see it differently. Hence the interview schedule had as far as possible to overcome these difficulties. Job descriptions and organization charts were studied, where available, before the interview. The final interview schedule for the jobholder included the following topics:

128

- Organizational location
- Key tasks, including whether the jobholder saw it as one job or a combination of different kinds of jobs
- Scope, including the number of subordinates and what was considered to be the best indication of the size of the job
- How job performance could be assessed
- What was distinctive about the job compared with any with similar titles in the organization
- The work that had to, or could, be done by the manager's unit, divided between work input, conversion and output
- What work could or could not be delegated and why it could not
- The decisions in which the manager got involved
- Membership of any work teams
- What the manager could do to limit disturbances to the unit
- The opportunities for innovation
- The kind of work that the manager could do outside the unit (for which a checklist was provided as well as comments being invited)
- The relative importance of different kinds of constraints (a checklist was also provided and comments invited here). What could be done to reduce any of them
- How the job compared with the manager's previous jobs in the opportunities for choice that it offered
- What the manager did that another jobholder might not do
- Choices in the range of contacts and in time spent with different types of contact

The usual length of the interviews was an hour and a half, though some were longer.

The interviews with the jobholder's boss took place after the interview with the jobholder. They were shorter: half to three-quarters of an hour. The interview schedule focused more directly upon the demands, constraints, and choices in the job, as it was found that it was easier to get this information from the boss. There were questions about particular kinds of choice, such as choices of emphasis, of innovation, of attracting or deflecting work, of risk-taking. These interviews were tape-recorded to provide a full record and to allow the author to listen to them.

Sample

The sample in the second stage of the study was 98 jobs, proportionately more at middle and senior management. About half the sample was a cross-section by function and level in a large company in the chemical industry. The others were in a variety of companies, including a cross-section of marketing and

129

finance in a large electronics company. The latter enabled some comparisons to be made with the large sample from the chemical company. The original aim of comparing jobs in similar functions and levels in two large companies failed because of difficulties in getting cooperation within the time available.

Analysis

The analysis was in two forms. The first was a study of the information on each of the 98 jobs to identify the overall demands, constraints, and choices; and to consider these for the input, conversion, and output stages of the unit's work, and separately for the work that the manager could do outside the unit. There was a more detailed analysis and comparison of the six pairs of jobs whose incumbents were observed. The aim of this first analysis was to try and get as complete a picture as possible of the job in terms of demands, constraints, and choices. This form of analysis proved more productive than the second, which was an attempt to make quantitative comparisons between the choices in different jobs, by function, level, contact type (see Stewart, 1976), and, within the limitations of the sample that could be obtained, by company. The choices identified in each job were coded and the computer was used for significance tests of the different factors mentioned above. This testing is the basis for the comments on organizational differences in Chapter 10. Otherwise, it has primarily been the information from the first analysis that has been used in writing this book.

Methods used in the district administrators' study

This study arose from an invitation from the King Edward's Hospital Fund for London, a large charity, to describe the nature of the job of the district administrator and the training implications of this description. This was a new post created in the reorganization of the National Health Service in 1974. The research design built on the experience of the previous studies and particularly upon that of 'A Classification of Choices'. The first stage of the research was to familiarize the research team with the nature of the job and to determine whether the study was likely to be useful. It also served as a pilot for the main study. It consisted of an observation of three district administrators for a week each. The observations, which were done by two of the researchers, followed a similar format to that for the previous project though the headings were adapted to suit the contacts in the job. The information was used to determine how the main part of the study should be designed. The three district administrators afterwards met with the researchers to discuss the job and the design of the research.

The pilot study included interviews with the principal members of the administrator's role set. This was not done in the main study because it was decided they did not add materially to the information and insights that could be obtained by interviewing and observing the administrators.

The sample

Interviews were held with a sample of 41 district administrators. This was about a fifth of the total number of district administrators. The sample was selected after studying the distribution of the different factors likely to affect the district administrators' work. These included the size of the district judged by three different criteria: number of hospitals, number of beds, and the percentage of acute to long-stay beds. In selecting a sample that provided a range on these characteristics we also took into account variations in other factors such as urban and rural, regional distribution, and teaching and non-teaching hospitals.

Interviews

The interview schedule was tested by the three researchers and the principal investigator in some preliminary interviews. It was decided to concentrate upon the work that the administrators had done recently. The last month was chosen as long enough to cover many, though not all, aspects of the job and recent enough to be recalled with the help of their detailed engagement books. The main interviews with 41 administrators were carried out by the three researchers. The interviewing schedule asked about the work done during the previous month under each of the main aspects of the job: managing administration; as a member of, and secretary to, the district management team; in relations with nursing and medical colleagues; in personnel management, and with the team of officers at the area and with the members of the area authority. The administrators were asked what, if anything, was abnormal about that past month. The interviews lasted three to seven hours so that considerable detail was collected about the work done. The administrators were also asked about what they were trying to achieve in each area of their job, about the satisfactions and frustrations of the job, and about what they felt they had achieved in the past year.

Kotter and Lawrence's (1974) concept of domains as the area in which the manager acts as if responsible was used to distinguish different ways of doing the job. The work reported by the administrators in the main areas of their job was compared and a provisional description of different types of administrator was developed. This was used as one of the criteria for selecting the administrators to be observed. The other criterion was length of time in the job. It was thought that it would be helpful in considering the training implications to look at those who had been in the job since it was created in 1974 and those who had been promoted within the last year or two.

Observations

In the main part of the study eight administrators were each observed for three days. The period was chosen to include a meeting of the district management team. The observation was recorded in a standard form that was similar to that used in the other studies. There was also a list of questions that the observer was asked to consider at the end of each day as a guide to thinking about the meaning of what had been observed. Observers made additional notes about events during the day that seemed relevant to understanding the job and the particular administrator's approach to it. The possible interpretations of the observations were discussed by the research team.

Seminars of administrators

A 24-hour seminar was held for those who had been observed, both to describe and to explore some of the findings. This seminar was seen as part of the research process. Later seminars were also held to provide feedback after the report was published.

Analysis

Separate analyses were made for each aspect of the job. The analysis took a number of forms: a numerical analysis of meetings attended; content analysis of work for the district management team; listing all the topics on which work was reported; tracing through actions on one problem over three days; and comparing the pattern of activities of different observed administrators. When all these, and other, forms of analysis had been made, time was spent considering possible interpretations of their significance. The last stage is as . important in a qualitative study as the earlier analyses, and should suggest fresh ways of analysing the material.

Comments on research methods used

A common feature of the two researches described above and of their predecessor, 'A Behavioural Classification of Managerial Jobs' is the use of a number of different research methods. The original study, no. 1 on Table A1.1, had used only diary-keeping. The advantages and limitations of this method have been described elsewhere (Stewart, 1979). Now that our understanding of the nature of managerial work has improved, the diary-keeping method is too limited for use except as a supplement to other methods—though some new and ingenious approach to what can be learnt from it may yet prove that statement to be wrong! Each of the methods used—open-ended interviews with the jobholder, with the jobholder's boss, and with members of the jobholder's role set; records of particular activities such as meetings attended; observations and group discussions—have their advantages and limitations. The advantages of one method can help to offset some of the limitations of the others. Together, they can help to give one a better understanding of what is being studied.

One new feature of the two studies discussed is a comparison of the behaviour of managers in similar jobs. It is a powerful way of increasing one's understanding of differences in managerial behaviour and of the flexibility in jobs. However, there remains the difficulty that the researcher is unlikely to understand fully how comparable the jobs are, given the demands and constraints that come from the particular relationships and from any other special features of the situation.

One commonly expressed reservation about observation is that it will alter what is being observed. Managers being observed, and those they are in contact with, will, it is argued, behave differently in the presence of an observer. There are reasons for thinking that this may not be a serious objection to the use of non-participant observation as a method of collecting information. The pace of most managerial work makes it hard for the manager, or for those whom he or she contacts, to behave differently. Those observed have all reported that within the first half-day or day they forgot the presence of the observer for most of the time. They also said that they did not think it altered what they did. The purpose of the observation, the manager's trust in the observer, and the novelty or otherwise of strangers, particularly strangers of a different sex, may all affect reactions to observation. A woman observing a production manager may, for instance, lead to more visitors who find a pretext to satisfy their curiosity, but such an effect will probably be short-lived. Some activities may not be undertaken when an observer is present, particularly those that a manager thinks might be criticized. However, my belief is that the manager's approach to his or her job is sufficiently ingrained, and the pace of work is often such, that what one observes provides a reasonably accurate picture of the nature of the work that the managers get involved in and of their style of working.

One problem in observation is the insight of the observer. What is wanted is someone who is both capable of observing analytically and detachedly and of thinking creatively about the meaning of what is being observed. An observer who does not have these characteristics can fill up an observer's format but cannot contribute to the understanding of what is being observed. Decisions about the research tools to be used should, therefore, take into account both the advantages and limitations of the different tools, and which ones are likely to be well used by those who are going to do the research.

Appendix 2

Illustrating the use of demands, constraints and choices in job descriptions

The job description should start, as in many job descriptions, with scope, key tasks, and organizational location. Following these, a description of the job in terms of its demands, constraints, and choices gives a more realistic description of the nature of the job than the customary job descriptions. The initial description of the job is omitted in the examples below to preserve anonymity.

Example 1   *Maintenance manager in urban local authority*

Demands

Overall

1. To ensure that equipment in the council's public buildings is serviced to a standard, and within a time period, that ensures that there are few complaints. Standards are listed in a handbook. The jobholder's attention to standards is monitored by the level of complaints and by political enquiries.
2. To ensure that there is no suspicion of bribery of the jobholder or his subordinates.

(*Note*: the overall demands are the criteria by which acceptable performance will be judged.)

Specific

1. Regular work that cannot be delegated
    (a) Answering letters from superiors and councillors
    (b) Authorizing expenditures above £X
    (c) Preparing annual budget, making manual checks on actual expenditure

135

    (d) Visiting sites to monitor work, though frequency and duration is a choice

    (e) Attending monthly meetings held by boss

    (f) Checking returns of work done

    (g) Ensuring that complaints are dealt with

2. Working relationships

    (a) Boss: geographically separate, which reduces the contact demands

    (b) Subordinates: contact primarily for advice about any politically sensitive problems and where the manager has superior technical expertise, but this will not be true for the work of all subordinates. Usually, subordinates will need little monitoring

    (c) Peers: little or no contact or demands

    (d) Contractors: relationship can be conducted formally and at arm's length

    (e) Clients: no demand for personal contact

3. Occasional work

    (a) To serve on working parties if particular expertise is asked for

    (b) To see visiting councillors

4. To be on 24-hour call for major emergencies

Constraints

On resources

1. Financial

    (a) To keep within the budget, which has a historical basis

    (b) A limit of £X on personal authorization

2. Staffing

    (a) Establishment control over direct labour: the jobholder can neither add to the numbers nor, in practice, decrease them

    (b) Regulations governing the use of contractors

    (c) Union agreements, which include nature of work to be done by different grades

3. Statutory (only the ones that are particularly relevant to this job)

    (a) Health and safety legislation

4. Organizational policies and procedures

    (a) Professional technical standards

    (b) Departmental handbook. This is very detailed: see comments under overall demands

5. Organizational structure

    (a) The main constraints come from the organizational separation of maintenance from the departments whose decisions affect it, together with insistence on formal contacts up the hierarchy and across

136

(b) These constraints are greatest for design, because design decisions affect maintenance requirements and for finance, administration, and establishment

Choices

Common choices (only the particular aspects in this job are included)

1. Emphasis
   (a) There is considerable choice between exercising only general supervisions or supervising closely. This includes:
   – Whether all incoming and outgoing mail is seen
   – Whether, and the extent to which, subordinates' technical decisions are monitored
   (b) The importance attached to the standard of service provided and the relative emphasis given to quality and speed
   (c) The importance attached to site visits and to the different purposes they can serve, e.g., monitoring and liaison with clients
2. Innovation
   (a) How much interest is taken in exploring different technical solutions to problems
   (b) The importance attached to trying to improve the organization of work

Distinctive choices

1. Boundary management
   (a) Trying to influence the design department to consider maintenance needs
2. Unit domain
   (a) No choice to try and change
3. Personal domain
   (a) Only choice is to seek to become known by senior officers for special expertise
4. Relationships
   (a) There is some choice in both who is seen and in how much time is spent with them
   (b) There is a choice in whether to make personal contact with clients, and whether to seek to offer a personalized, helpful service
   (c) There is a choice in whether to see contractors in the hope of getting a better service, or to avoid contact to keep the relationship a very formal one. The desire to avoid any suspicion of bribery may favour this option

Comment

It is a job where the choices are limited more by the constraints over what can be done than by the pressure of demands. The main constraints are those stemming from organizational policies about the use of formal channels of communication between departments and the regulations governing the work of contractors. Union agreements and union attitudes to what work should be done are also important constraints.

Example 2 Technical director in medium-sized subsidiary in metal manufacture

The parent company exercises mainly financial control, and broad product definition.

Demands

Overall

1. To ensure that the department produces accurate and speedy quotations and designs
2. To participate in policy decisions

Specific

1. As head of department
   (a) To respond to requests for technical advice from subordinates
   (b) To sign authorizations
2. As a member of the top management team
   (a) To attend meetings
   (b) To contribute his/her specialist knowledge to policy decisions
3. Working relationships
   (a) To work closely with his/her boss contributing technical expertise as required
   (b) To respond to key customers who expect direct contact with jobholder
   (c) To respond to requests for specialist help from accounts, sales, and production
   (d) To respond to technical queries from head office
4. Time
   (a) The volume of work to be done and the shortage of technically qualified staff imposes considerable demands on the technical director's time

138

Constraints

On resources

1. Financial
   (a) Company annual budget: refer any excess expenditure
2. Staffing
   (a) Shortage of technically qualified staff to undertake development

Statutory

No distinctive constraints

Organizational policies and procedures

No distinctive constraints

Technological

Technical feasibility of designs

Attitudes

The interest and knowledge of the other directors affects work at the boundaries between departments

Choices

Common choices

1. Emphasis
   (a) Amount of delegation within limitations of technical expertise
   (b) The attention given to development
   (c) Relative importance attached to helping subordinates, working with fellow directors, and external contacts
2. Innovation
   (a) Wide choice both in organization of own department and in which developments to initiate to help other departments

Distinctive choices

Much of the job is what the jobholder makes it. There is a choice in the depth and variety of involvement, particularly in work outside own department

1. Work-sharing
   (a) Wide choice in the nature and extent of help to other departments, and how far the jobholder gets involved in their problems
2. Expertise
   (a) Choice in making visible and contributing expertise to the parent company

Appendix 3
Exercises for the individual manager

Readers who wish to improve their effectiveness will find the exercises on pages 142–158 a good way of applying the ideas in Chapter 11. All the exercises have been used in courses with a wide variety of managers from different functions and organizations. The first five exercises are to help you to analyse your job; the last four are to help you to review how you do it. The first four exercises can be done rapidly; the remainder will take much longer, but the experience of other managers suggests that they can be very helpful.

Exercise 1   To determine whether, and if so how far, your job requires strategic thinking

Most jobs offer some choice in *what* work is done by the jobholder. The more choices there are, the greater the need for strategic thinking. It is also needed in jobs where there are choices in what work is produced by the manager's unit.

The place for your job on the diagram for exercise 1 shows how much need there is for strategic thinking. If it is in the top left-hand corner you have little scope for strategic thinking about what you should do; the more it is towards the bottom right-hand corner, the more important it is for you to think strategically.

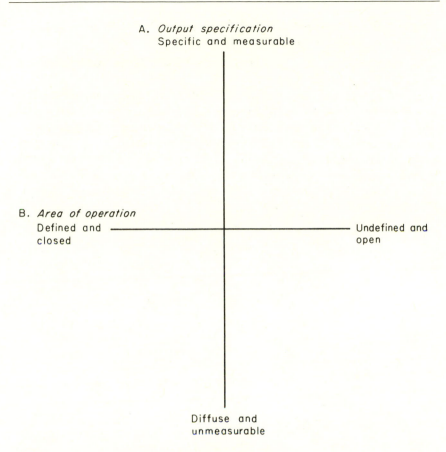

A. *Output specification*
Specific and measurable

B. *Area of operation*
Defined and closed

Undefined and open

Diffuse and unmeasurable

Fig. App. 3.1   Exercise 1. Need for strategic thinking

For A axis, consider:

– The extent to which the work for which you are responsible has a specified output, which is measurable. The greater the number of specific measures, and the more frequent they are, the higher up the scale.
– At the lower end consider what, if any, of the work for which you are responsible can be measured.

For B axis, consider:

– Whether the work for which you are responsible is (1) well-defined, (2) capable of change by you, (3) whether, in addition to your key responsibilities, you can take on other work.

143

Exercise 2 To consider the demands upon you to spend time supervising your subordinates

(The words 'influencing' or 'learning' can be substituted for supervising if you prefer it.)

Consider where your job should be placed on the diagram for exercise 2: the more it is towards the top left-hand corner, the less time you will need to spend with subordinates; the more it is towards the bottom right-hand corner, the more time you should spend with them. Compare the need to influence your subordinates, shown by the position on the diagram, with the time that you actually spend, preferably checking this by keeping a diary.

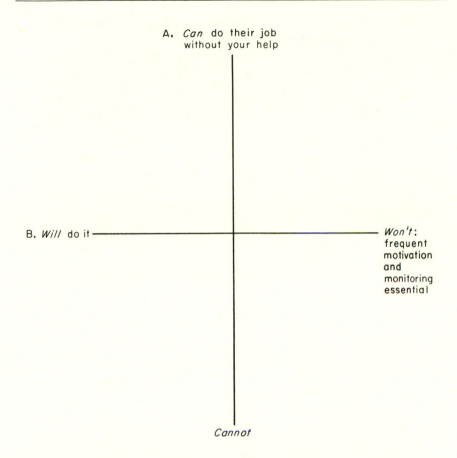

A. *Can* do their job
without your help

B. *Will* do it ──────────────────────── *Won't*:
frequent
motivation
and
monitoring
essential

Cannot

Fig. App. 3.2   Exercise 2. Influencing needs in the job: 1. Immediate subordinates

For position on A axis, consider:

– Knowledge, experience and access to necessary information
– Number of your subordinates with above

For position on B axis, consider:

– Intrinsic motivation of their jobs
– Other factors likely to make for high or low motivation

145

Exercise 3   To consider the need to influence your boss and people in other parts of the organization

The position of your job on the vertical axis of the diagram for exercise 3 will show whether what you can do in your job is dependent upon the character of your boss and upon how he or she regards you. The more boss-dependent you are, the more important it is for you to try and please your boss, particularly if you want to be given more scope in your job.

The position of your job on the B axis shows whether you need to try and influence people in other parts of the organization. The higher your dependence upon them, the more effort you should give to boundary management (see Chapter 3).

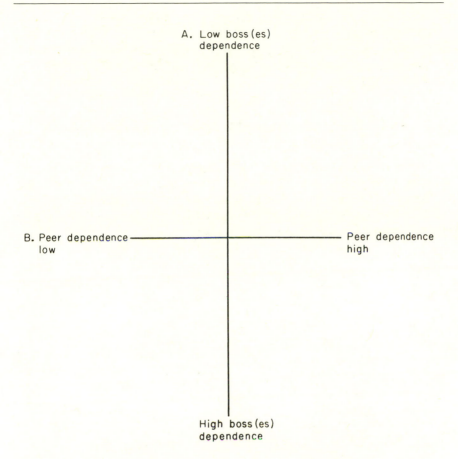

Fig. App. 3.3   Exercise 3. Influencing needs in the job: 2. Other contacts within the organization (parent company)

For position on A axis, consider:

– Whether the scope that you have in your job is dependent upon your making a good impression upon your boss(es). If the scope that you have is not affected by your boss's opinion of you, score at the top end (low). The more it is affected, the further down you should score on the axis.

For position on B axis, consider:

– Whether you can run your unit (e.g., section, department, branch, division,

147

etc.) without having to influence people in other units to give you services and supplies, or to accept yours (low peer dependence), or whether what you can do is wholly dependent upon your capacity to influence them to supply you/help you, and to be willing to accept your output (high peer dependence).

Exercise 4   To consider the need to influence people outside the organization

The exercise is relevant only for those who must have contacts with people outside their organization. The more your job is placed towards the top left-hand corner on the diagram for exercise 4, the less is the need for you to seek to influence people outside the organization; the more it is towards the right-hand bottom corner, the greater is the need.

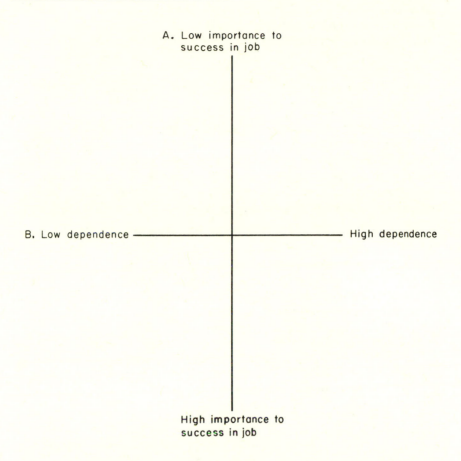

A. Low importance to
   success in job

B. Low dependence ———————————————————— High dependence

High importance to
success in job

Fig. App. 3.4   Exercise 4. Influencing needs in the job: 3. External contacts (outside
                the parent organization)

For position on A axis, consider:

– How far successful influence of people outside the organization is a major
  determinant of whether you are effective in your job (the bottom end of the
  scale), or whether this is only a minor aspect of the job (the top end of the
  scale)

For position on B axis, consider:

– At low end, whether your external contacts want something from you, that

149

is, whether you are in a strong position; at the high end, you are in a weak bargaining/influencing position
– Take into account the different kinds of external contacts you *must* have

Exercise 5   To consider the demands, constraints, and choices in your job

This is the most time-consuming, but potentially the most rewarding, exercise. To do it you may find it helpful to reread Chapter 1. Make a list of the demands, constraints, and choices of your job. You will probably find it easiest to do this for each of the major parts of the job. If you have done the previous exercises you will find that this helps you in deciding some of the demands. It is useful to consider demands from the following sources:

1. *Subordinates*   The minimum time that must be spent with subordinates to avoid penalties. (Exercise 2 is an important guide to the demands here)
2. *Boss*   What your boss expects and you cannot ignore without penalty
3. *Peers*   The requests for services, information, or help from people outside your unit that you cannot ignore or delegate without penalty
4. *People outside the organization*   Requests for services, information, or help that you cannot ignore or delegate without penalty
5. *Administrative demands*
   – Returns, budgets, and other procedures that cannot be ignored or wholly delegated
   – Meetings that cannot be skipped.

In deciding on the demands under each of the headings above you will need to consider how serious are the penalties for not doing them.
Chapter 1 (page 5) outlines some of the more important constraints that you should consider in listing those that apply to your job. If you can, get someone else to check your view of what your demands and constraints are.
The previous chapters described the choices that you should consider, but you may find it convenient to consider them under the following headings.

1. *Within your unit*   Delegation; emphasis on different aspects; change in the nature of the work; innovation in methods; changes in organization; technology; leadership style
2. *Within the management team(s)*   Influence; sharing of tasks; the role you play
3. *Boundary management*   To protect unit from disturbance; to permit changes in outputs or inputs
4. *Upwards*   To influence boss, other seniors; delegating up; getting more delegated down
5. *Elsewhere in organization*   Working parties; becoming known as an expert

150

6. *Outside the organization*   Professional contacts; developing network; bargaining strategy

Decide what are the most important choices in the job for it to be done effectively.

Exercise 6   Reviewing the choices of your work pattern

The aim of this exercise is to help you to improve the way in which you organize, or fail to organize, your time. It does not seek to cover all the things that can be said about the effective use of time, but it asks you to identify and appraise the choices that you make in the pattern of your day and week.

Your should have kept a record of your activities and contacts for this exercise. The diagram for exercise 6 illustrates a simple form that you could use for this purpose, to which you should make adjustments to give you any specific information that you want. Keep the diagram for at least a week, preferably longer. It should be kept as you go along rather than filled in later. Make a determined effort to keep it accurately for at least one day. The last column of the diary is for you to put a tick for a brief episode, usually a short discussion that you do not have time to record properly.

Check the number of episodes in a day, particularly the day(s) where you really tried to keep the diary accurately. You can count meetings and an uninterrupted spell dealing with correspondence, as one episode; otherwise a new episode starts whenever you switch your attention from one subject or person to another.

Looking at your diary, consider the following:

– How fragmented is your day, and how much variation is there from one day to another? As a guide to the fragmentation in other managers' days, we have observed from 10 to 120 episodes in a day.
– On most days do you have at least half an hour uninterrupted?
– If not, do you think you would work more effectively if you had?
– If the answer is 'yes', keep the diary for another day or two when you are busy and note how many of the interruptions are caused by yourself, and how many are ones from other people that could be avoided.
– How available do you need to be, when, and to whom? You may pride yourself on always being available. This may be a choice rather than a demand. Consider the price that you are paying for this choice and ask whether it is worth it.
– How much time do you spend in meetings? Is there some choice here? In some jobs they may be inescapable, but in others there is a choice, one that is often unrecognized.

Change of activity	
Other external to co.	
Other internal	
Boss	
Subs	
Face to face	
Tel.	
Alone	
Brief description	
Time	
Day	

Fig. App. 3.6   Diary

Exercise 7   To appraise your own demands, constraints and choices

Go through the entries in the diary that you kept for exercise 6, marking which ones were a choice in the sense that you did not have to do that, not merely that you did not have to do it *then*.

Using the diary as an aid, identify your personal demands, constraints and choices, that is, the work that you treat as a demand though another incumbent might not do so; the constraints that stem from your attitudes, abilities, or status rather than intrinsically from the job, and the work that you choose to do.

Now look at the choices that you listed in exercise 5 and consider whether any of these are more important than the ones that you are currently taking. Take into account the relevant questions on the checklist about effectiveness (Chapter 11, pages 110–111).

Review your constraints. Are they all as definite obstacles as you see them? Take the more important ones in turn and ask which ones you see as necessary or inevitable and which as frustrating obstacles. Consider what could be done to try and overcome the latter and who might be able to help. You may find exercise 9 helpful here.

Exercise 8   Identify your personal priorities (your agenda)

In Chapter 11 we discussed the value of understanding what your own *personal* goals and priorities are and said that we found that many managers did not realize that these were not identical with any formal job objectives. List your own goals and priorities. In doing so consider what is distinctive about how you do your job. This can help you to identify your own goals.

You may find it helpful to list your goals and priorities under such headings as:

– For the output of your unit
– The changes that you want to get accomplished
– For your relationships, including how you wish to be seen by others
– For the climate of your organization
– For your personal development
– For your own satisfaction
– In the relationships of your work and private life

Examples of the personal goals and priorities of one of the managers whom we observed are given on page 156.

If you find this difficult, it probably means that your selection of priorities is instinctive and short-term. Consider whether you might not be more effective if you selected your priorities more consciously and had a strategy that looked further ahead. If the first exercise showed that your job required strategic thinking, you should have a clear view of your goals and priorities.

Melting Shop Manager B—Age 36

Production

To ensure that the quality of product produced matches the orders

To keep an adequate balance between output, quality, and cost, in a period of recession, with a focus on the quality specified for the orders

To work towards the successful commissioning of new production methods

To try out different methods, materials, and equipment that can improve overall performance and monitor the results

Relationships, organization and IR

To involve everyone who can affect the work's performance so that they understand what contribution they can make

To ensure that everyone understands and uses the contributions that others can make, by acting as a referee

To raise the confidence of young staff while also educating them

To gain and retain the respect of the workforce

To establish good working relationships with trade union officials

To work towards further autonomy in the management of his department

Personal and career development

To maintain and improve his own technical knowledge

To establish professional contacts outside the organization

*Exercise 9   Reviewing your network and the effectiveness of your
relationships*

Using a diagram like that illustrated for this exercise (page 158), go though the
following steps.

1. Write in all the people or groups of people that can affect how effective you
   are in the job
2. Rate each one from 1 to 3 for their importance to you in getting your job
   done effectively
3. Rate on a scale from − 3 to + 3 the extent to which each person or group of
   people helps or hinders you in getting your job done
4. Note how the rating in (3) compared with that for importance
5. Now look at those you have marked with a minus sign and consider what
   you can do to improve the effectiveness of the relationship
6. Are there any other people with whom it would be helpful to have personal
   contact? If so, put them in an outer circle and review how you might
   achieve this

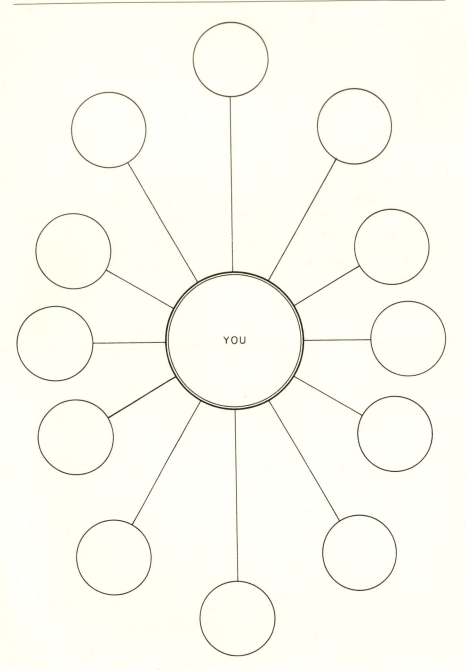

Fig. App. 3.9   Analysis of contacts

References

Armstrong, Lord (1977) 'The individual, the enterprise and the state: a personal view', in *The Individual, the Enterprise and the State*, R. I. Tricker (ed.), p. 32. Associated Business Programmes, London. First presented at a seminar at the Oxford Centre for Management Studies.

Bales, R. F. (1950) *Interaction Process Analysis*, Addison-Wesley, Reading, Mass.

Bass, Bernard, M. Burger, and C. Philip, in collaboration with Robert Doktor and Gerald V. Barrett (1979) *Assessment of Managers: An International Comparison*, Free Press, New York.

Belbin, R. M. (1981) *Management Teams: Why They Succeed or Fail*, Heinemann, London; Halstead Press, New York.

Belbin, R. M., B. R. Aston, and R. D. Mottram (1976) 'Building effective management teams', *Journal of General Management*, 3, 3.

Burgoyne, J. and R. Stuart (1976) 'The nature, use and acquisition of managerial skills and other attributes', *Personnel Review*, 5, 4, 19–29.

Burns, Tom and G. M. Stalker (1961) *The Management of Innovation*, Tavistock, London.

Carlson, S. (1951) *Executive Behaviour: A Study of the Work Load and the Working Methods of Managing Directors*, Strömbergs, Stockholm.

Drucker, P. (1967) *The Effective Executive*, Heinemann, London.

Fowles, J. (1970) *The Aristos*, New American Library, New York.

Graves, Desmond (1973) 'The impact of culture upon managerial attitudes, beliefs and behavior in England and France', in *Management Research: A Cross-Cultural Perspective*, Desmond Graves (ed.), Elsevier, Amsterdam.

Hackman, R. T. (1969) 'Towards understanding the role of tasks in behavioral research', *Acta Psychologica*, 31, 97–128.

Hemphill, J. K. (1960) *Dimensions of Executive Positions*, Bureau of Business Research, Research Monograph 98, Ohio State University, Columbus.

Hofstede, Geert (1980) *Cultures Consequences*, Sage, Beverley Hills, California.

Katz, Robert L. (1955) 'Skills of an effective administrator', *Harvard Business Review*; revised version September–October 1974, 90–102.

Knibbs, John (1975) 'The manager and colleague relationships—training in trading skills?' *Industrial Training International*, 10, 7, 224–5.

Kotter, John (1982) *The General Manager*, in press.

Kotter, J. P. and P. Lawrence (1974) *Mayors in Action: Five Studies in Urban Governance*, John Wiley, New York.

Lombardo, M. M. and M. W. McCall, Jr (1981) 'Looking Glass Inc.: An organizational simulation', in *Leadership: Beyond Establishment Views*, J. G. Hunt, M. Sekaran and C. A. Schriesheim (eds), Southern Illinois University Press, Carbondale, Ill.

Machin, J., R. Stewart and C. Hales (1981) *Managerial Effectiveness*, Gower, Farnborough, Hants.

Marshall J. and R. Stewart (1981a and b) 'Manager's job perceptions: Parts 1 and 2', *Journal of Management Studies*, 18, 2 and 3.

Miles, Robert J. (1980) *Macro-Organizational Behavior*, Goodyear, Santa Monica, California.

Mintzberg, H. (1973) *The Nature of Managerial Work*, Harper and Row, New York. 1980 edition, Prentice Hall, Englewood Cliffs, N.J.

Rapoport, Robert N. (1970) *Mid Career Development: Research Perspectives on a Developmental Community for Senior Administrators*, Tavistock, London.

Sayles, L. R. (1964) *Managerial Behavior: Administration in Complex Organizations*, McGraw-Hill, New York.

Schein, E. H. (1975) 'How "career anchors" hold executives to their career paths', *Personnel*, 52, 11–24.

Schein, E. H. (1978) *Career Dynamics: Matching Individual and Organizational Needs*, Addison-Wesley, Reading, Mass.

Stewart, R. (1967) *Managers and their Jobs*, Macmillan, London.

Stewart, R. (1976) *Contrasts in Management: A Study of the Different Types of Managers' Jobs: Their Demands and Choices*, McGraw-Hill, Maidenhead, Berks.

Stewart, R. (1979) 'The Manager's Contacts: Demand or Choice?' *Journal of European Industrial Training*, 3, 4, 2–5.

Stewart, R. (1981) 'The relevance of some studies of managerial work and behavior to leadership studies', in *Leadership: Beyond Establishment Views*, J. G. Hunt, M. Sekaran and C. A. Schriesheim (eds), Southern Illinois University Press, Carbondale, Ill.

Stewart, R., P. Smith, J. Blake and P. Wingate (1980) *The District Administrator in the National Health Service*, King Edward's Hospital Fund for London, London; distributed by Pitman Medical.

Tornow, W. and P. Pinto (1976) 'The development of a managerial job taxonomy: a system for describing, classifying and evaluating executive positions', *Journal of Applied Psychology*, 61, 410–18.

Index